How to Start and Run a Successful Consulting Business

How to Start and Run a Successful Consulting Business

GREGORY KISHEL AND PATRICIA KISHEL

John Wiley & Sons, Inc.

New York   Chichester   Brisbane   Toronto   Singapore

Copyright © 1996 by Gregory Kishel and Patricia Kishel.
Published by John Wiley & Sons, Inc.

This publication is designed to provide accurate and authoritative information in regard to the subject matter covered. It is sold with the understanding that the publisher is not engaged in rendering legal, accounting, or other professional services. If legal advice or other expert assistance is required, the services of a competent professional person should be sought.

Library of Congress Cataloging-in-Publication Data

Kishel, Gregory F., 1946–
    How to start and run a successful consulting business / by Gregory and Patricia Kishel.
      p.   cm.
    Rev. ed. of: Cashing in on the consulting boom, c1985.
    Includes bibliographical references.
    ISBN 0-471-12544-X (cloth : alk. paper). — ISBN 0-471-12545-8 (paper : alk. paper)
    1. Business consultants.   I. Kishel, Patricia Gunter, 1948–
II. Kishel, Gregory F., 1946–   Cashing in on the consulting boom.
III. Title.
HD69.C6K53 1996
658.4′6′0681—dC20   95-30481
                                                      CIP

Printed in the United States of America

10 9 8 7 6 5 4 3 2 1

Contents

PREFACE

This book is designed to help you build your career as an independent consultant and turn your knowledge and experience into a profitable business. By definition, a *consultant* is someone who works independently, providing the specialized services and advice that organizations and individuals need to achieve their goals. The most important product any consultant has to sell is his or her ideas and information, skills, and abilities. In effect, as an independent consultant you will be paid for what you know and can do for others.

The consulting industry is one of the fastest growing business sectors worldwide with new opportunities emerging continually in hundreds of different fields. Whatever your area of expertise—engineering or employee relations, computers or customer service—there's likely to be a demand for your consulting abilities. Such occupations as sales trainer, health-care specialist, electronics expert, investment counselor, and marketing researcher illustrate the diversity within the consulting industry. Among those who have embarked on successful consulting careers are managers and technicians, retirees eager to profit from their years of experience, college professors and recent graduates, former government employees, and career changers.

As active consultants ourselves, we have structured this book to provide the answers to your questions on matters ranging from "Which field should I choose?" to "How can I generate more income?" Covering all aspects of becoming an independent consultant, the book offers step-by-step advice on setting up your business and determining fees, promoting your services and maintaining good client relations, obtaining repeat business and referrals, selling to the government, entering foreign markets, and more.

Our goal in writing *How to Start and Run a Successful Consulting Business* was to show you how to make the most out of your talents, putting them to work for you and your clients. Drawing on our own experiences as management consultants and business writers, we wanted to share with you the things that we've learned along the way that can add to your success. In addition to telling you about what goes into being a consultant, we have focused on the consulting industry itself: where the opportunities are, who uses consultants (and why), and the various situations you are likely to encounter. Whether you're just starting your consulting business or already running it, you'll find in this book the information you need to make it succeed.

1

Who Needs Consultants?

Who needs consultants? "Who *doesn't* need consultants?" Consulting-industry revenues are increasing at a dramatic rate. Projects are becoming bigger, longer, and much more complex. As organizations and individuals attempt to adapt to new technologies and a constantly changing environment, consultants are taking on greater roles. No longer viewed as a luxury, consultants have become a necessity. Now it appears that virtually everyone needs the help of one kind of consultant or another. Government agencies, businesses, and nonprofit organizations are turning to outside consultants with increasing frequency both to keep fixed costs down and to obtain the most up-to-date information. At the same time, individuals now seek the advice of consultants on personal and professional matters ranging from planning finances to choosing the right college, from charting a career to designing a physical-fitness regimen.

WHY CLIENTS HIRE CONSULTANTS

There are many factors behind the current consulting boom. Chief among them is the complexity of our day-to-day lives. Regardless of their capabilities, organizations and individuals are finding it difficult, or impossible, to accomplish their goals single-handedly. For example, if a business wants to expand its advertising coverage, it has thousands of media outlets from which to choose, including over 50,000 different newspapers and magazines and more than 24,000 radio and television stations. Add to this the fact that as organizations continue to downsize and streamline their operations, there's a greater need for outsiders to do that work. Individuals need help, too. For example, as people become more health conscious and concerned about the artificial additives in their foods, it takes more than a passing knowledge of the seven basic food groups to plan their diets. To make the right decisions, complete tasks properly, use resources efficiently, and take advantage of existing opportunities, expert advice or assistance is often needed.

Situations That Require Consultants

Each of the following situations commonly requires the services of a consultant, and each represents a type of problem that consultants are frequently called on to solve.

The Client Has a Deadline to Meet

One of the main reasons for hiring a consultant is that the client simply can't finish what needs to be done in the time available for its completion. A business that needs to line up additional distributors in time for a key buying season is an example of this situation. A government agency that has to gather specific research information for an upcoming Senate hearing is another. So is the individual who must have his or her tax return ready to file on April 15. In these situations, the client needs someone who can start work immediately and has the ability to achieve the desired outcome.

The Client Lacks the Expertise to Do the Job

Consultants are often called in when the client is faced with a situation that requires specialized skills, training, or knowledge. Few organizations and individuals possess the necessary qualifications to make all the decisions or perform all the tasks that require their attention. Using consultants is a way to obtain the expertise they need. For example, an organization that wants to install a more efficient phone system is likely to engage the services of a telecommunications consultant. An individual who has reached a career impasse might seek out a career-development consultant for help in deciding what action to take.

The Client Has a Personnel Shortage

Consultants can be a cost-effective means of combating temporary personnel shortages. Rather than having to go through a lengthy process to find, recruit, hire, and train a new employee, the client can simply hire a consultant. Speeding up the selection process in this way saves the client not only time, but also money. Even when the consultant's fee is higher than an employee's salary would be, there can still be a significant savings because the consultant is not eligible to receive the benefits (vacation, holiday, and sick pay; insurance; pension; and other compensation) that employees receive in addition to their salaries. These benefits typically amount to more than 35 percent of a worker's annual salary.

The Client Needs an Objective Viewpoint

Good consultants bring more than expertise to their assignments; they bring an objective viewpoint. Whereas the client or the client's staff may be used to seeing the situation in a certain way, the consultant sees it without preconceived ideas. This objectivity can be invaluable, enabling the consultant to come up with innovative solutions to problems and to make unbiased recommendations.

Unlike employees, who are often afraid of losing their jobs or of alienating their co-workers, consultants have no such fears. Because the consultant doesn't stand to win or lose on the basis of the changes that are implemented, the client feels confident of getting an honest opinion.

The Client Wants to Capitalize on the Consultant's Credibility

When a recommendation or assessment comes from an outside consultant, it generally has more credibility than if it had come from an employee, relative, or friend. The higher the consultant's level of expertise and objectivity, the higher his or her credibility. Having a certified public accountant examine a corporation's accounting records each year not only meets a legal requirement, but also reassures shareholders that the organization is being truthful with them. Hiring a real estate appraiser to determine the current market value of a home serves a similar purpose, in this case verifying what the property is really worth.

The Client Wants to Avoid Going through Channels

The services of a consultant are often desirable when a client wants to get quick results or protect confidential information. Rather than going through normal channels, which might be more time-consuming and involve more people, the client brings in a consultant to do the job. For example, a business that wants to win government contracts might hire a government procurement consultant with contacts in Washington. The consultant is in a better position to find out about contract opportunities than someone who is unfamiliar with the way the government operates. Other types of consultants that businesses use when they want to avoid going through channels include consultants in such fields as investigation, security systems, new-product development, marketing research, new ventures, and banking.

The Client Wants to Avoid a Conflict

To avoid conflicts within their own businesses, it's not uncommon for clients to hire consultants to carry out controversial or politically charged assignments. Overseeing a company's reorganization plan, negotiating the terms of a union contract, rating a department's efficiency level, and choosing between one strategy and another are all examples of this. By having a consultant make the decision or perform the task, clients are able to disassociate themselves from the proceedings. Thus, any ill feelings that result will be directed toward the consultant rather than the client. Later, once the consultant has left, it will be easier for all parties involved to resume their normal working relationships.

The Client Is Experiencing a Crisis

Not surprisingly, clients also expect consultants to bail them out of trouble when a crisis hits. Consultants might be used in many types of crises: The client is facing bankruptcy; consumer groups are complaining; quality control levels have dropped; additional capital is needed; a lawsuit has been filed against the client; the client's health is endangered; an important decision must be made. Whatever the nature of the crisis, the client needs someone to step in and turn the situation around, successfully dealing with the problem and saving the day.

The Client Wants a Second Opinion

In many instances, a consultant is hired simply to prove (or disprove) the client's previous findings. The need for a second opinion isn't just confined to the medical field; having the benefit of an additional viewpoint can be advantageous in a number of fields. Consultants who are frequently asked to provide second opinions include medical and legal consultants, engineering experts, management consultants, marketing researchers, tax advisers, and public opinion pollsters.

The Client Doesn't Wish to Perform the Task

Sometimes even though the client could perform the task, he or she prefers not to do it. Perhaps it isn't cost-effective for the client to perform the task, or the client finds the task distasteful. Perhaps the client wants the status that comes from using a professional to carry out the assignment, or the client has a budget surplus and must "use it or lose it." Under these circumstances, a consultant's services allow the client to accomplish the task while satisfying a personal need.

SERVICES CONSULTANTS PROVIDE

The types of services that consultants provide run the gamut from furnishing clients with information and advice to actually supervising or performing the work that needs to be done. Following are some of the more common services that consultants provide.

Researching

Consultants often help clients by gathering information and conducting in-depth studies, such as researching the impact of proposed legislation or consumers' reactions to a new product. Depending on the scope of the research assignment, this can involve obtaining *secondary data* or *primary data*. Secondary data is information that is already in print or is readily available from recognized sources. Primary data is information based on first-hand observations, surveys, or experiments.

Advising

The service for which consultants are best known is advising: making recommendations on the specific courses of action that clients should follow. Recognizing the value of expert advice, many businesses have gone so far as to establish permanent advisory boards to aid their top managers and corporate directors. Individuals also have been quick to hire consultants, asking them for advice on how to advance their careers, improve their financial standings, and enjoy life more.

Planning

One of the consulting services that has been in great demand in recent years is planning, specifically the area of strategic planning. In an effort to meet competitive challenges and keep pace with rapidly changing technologies, businesses are intent on devising strategies, or overall plans, for researching their objectives. Some consulting firms have become so adept at helping clients set objectives and develop the policies and procedures for attaining them that they no longer offer any other types of services.

Evaluating

Sometimes, what the client really wants is for the consultant to rate the effectiveness of an existing method or approach to a problem. A consultant might be asked to evaluate, among other things, a client's current advertising campaign, inventory control system, employee compensation plan, office layout, or physical-fitness program.

Training

As jobs become more specialized and employees must continually upgrade their skills, the need for consultants' training services increases. Consultants are meeting this need by developing specialized training programs that can enable employees to improve their technical, human-relations, and administrative skills. Through personal instruction, audio and video materials, workbooks, and computer simulations, consultants help employees be more productive in their current jobs and prepare them for advanced positions.

Supervising

In addition to advising clients on the best ways to achieve their goals, many consultants also assume the role of supervisor, making sure that their recommendations are carried out correctly. This can entail supervising the client's staff, the consultant's own staff, or independent contractors. The consultants who normally provide clients with supervision services include architectural and engineering consultants, interior designers, caterers, and conference planners.

CONSULTING TRENDS

What does the future hold for the consulting industry? Which types of consulting services will be in demand? How will consultants fare in comparison to others in the labor force? The answers to these questions and more depend largely on the changes that occur in the economy, the political environment, technology, and our lifestyles in general.

The Economy

The consulting industry, as a whole, is one of the few industries that is virtually unaffected by economic cycles. When the economy is strong, consultants do well because clients can easily afford to hire them. When the economy is weak, consultants still do well because clients become more dependent on them for their services. Within the consulting industry itself, the demand for particular consulting services can fluctuate. For example, during periods of high employment, the demand for specialists in employee selection, training, and relocation rises as businesses compete with one another for the most qualified workers. Conversely, the demand for career-development consultants is likely to drop, due to the widespread availability of jobs.

The Political Environment

The power of our political institutions to enact legislation, tighten or loosen regulations, and increase or decrease government spending can have a profound effect on the demand for consultants. Any change in the laws creates a demand for consultants who can interpret the change and advise clients on how to comply with the new law. For example, stricter antipollution regulations result in a greater demand for pollution-control consultants; weaker regulations cause the demand to diminish. Budget cutbacks in one area can force those agencies that have been affected to hire fewer consultants. On the other hand, agencies whose budgets have been expanded are able to hire more consultants.

Technology

The development of new technologies creates a demand for consultants who are familiar with the technologies and can assist clients in implementing them. Computers, electronics, communications, medicine, engineering, manufacturing, and agriculture are just a few of the fields that are undergoing large-scale technological changes. Even the arts aren't immune to the impact of modern technology, as evidenced by the growing interest in computer-generated graphics, holograms, and interactive video.

Lifestyles

Individual lifestyles must also be taken into consideration. As the number of working women and two-paycheck families continues to grow, so does the demand for consulting services. Instead of taking the time to gather information themselves or perform various tasks,

individuals rely more heavily on consultants. Some of the consultants who have benefited from this lifestyle change include interior
designers, party-entertainment specialists, financial planners, and
investment counselors. Our society's increasing health conscious-
ness has also created opportunities for consultants, especially those
in the nutrition and physical-fitness fields.

In addition to monitoring these areas to detect consulting trends,
it's important to keep a close watch on your competitors. Who are
they? What types of services do they offer? What are their fees? How
do they solicit consulting business? Keeping track of the competition will provide you with a better understanding of your industry
and will help you identify new consulting trends.

2

Picking Your Field

Most consultants discover early in their careers that it's not possible to be all things to all people. Attempting to be the jack-of-all-trades of consulting is to invite disaster. For one thing, knowledge that is highly valued in one industry may be of little importance in a different industry. Ironic as it seems, the very qualities that enable you to excel in a particular area can hold you back in another. To achieve success as a consultant, you must define what it is you have to offer and how your experience can best be applied. What you are able to accomplish, how others see you, and how you see yourself hinge, in part, on picking the consulting field that is right for you.

You may already have identified the consulting field you would like to enter, or you may be investigating several alternatives. In either case, how can you be certain of making the best choice? Will the type of consulting practice you elect to start provide the financial and emotional rewards you seek? Even though there are no sure things in business, you *can* increase the probability of your success by taking certain factors into consideration, including the economy, the political environment, technology, client needs and preferences, and the competition. The single most important factor of all, though, is you. Just because a consulting business is right for a friend or colleague doesn't mean it is right for you. Nor is specializing in the "hot" consulting topic of the moment necessarily the answer. To be the right choice, the consulting field you pick must truly reflect your interests and qualifications.

INTERESTS

In weighing the pros and cons of the various consulting fields from which to choose, start by asking yourself, "What really interests me?" For now anyway, set aside the issues of qualifications and the needs of the marketplace and examine your own needs. Selecting a consulting field that matches your interests is crucial because you're not just investing a sum of money or even time in a business; you're investing part of yourself. It's vital that you enjoy what you do and feel challenged and excited by the consulting assignments you are asked to perform. This is the number one prerequisite for attaining professional satisfaction and giving clients the quality of service they deserve.

The list that follows should help you get in tune with your own interests. Rather than being an exhaustive catalog of every interest imaginable, this list is intended to stimulate your thinking. Once you've thought about which of these interests—and any others you want to add—relate to you, write them down. The more interests that you can incorporate into your consulting activities, the better. For instance, if you are interested in working with people in groups and enjoy problem solving, researching, and training, you should pick a consulting field that will allow you to pursue these interests. Three possible fields are employee selection and training, career guidance, and small-business development.

Types of Interests

Working independently
Working with people in
    groups

Working with numbers and
    statistics
Working with computers

Working with machines
Working with your hands
Working outdoors
Working indoors
Researching
Analyzing
Managing
Organizing
Problem solving
Investing
Creating or inventing

Designing
Drawing or painting
Writing
Speaking
Training
Traveling
Enhancing people's personal
  appearance
Enhancing people's health
Enhancing people's quality of
  life

QUALIFICATIONS

Listing your interests was the first step toward picking a consulting field. The next step is to take a personal inventory of your qualifications: the experience, education, and skills on which you can draw. By examining your strengths and weaknesses in each of these areas, you can gain a clearer idea of the various fields for which you are currently suited.

Experience

Experience is the best teacher. To determine what you can do as a consultant, start by looking at what you have already done in the past. Write down the jobs you have held, the tasks you have performed, and the activities in which you have taken part. In going over your experience, don't limit yourself to just paid work experience. Be sure to include volunteer and life experience as well. If you served on a fund-raising committee for a charitable organization, include that. If you were a "military brat" as a child and have lived in several foreign countries, that should be included, too.

The goal here isn't just to write out a list of job titles. It's to get at the essence of what each job entailed and the experience you gained in carrying it out. It's also to increase your awareness of the experience you have acquired that's unrelated to work. For instance, suppose you have worked in advertising, volunteered to help in a political campaign, and are an amateur photographer. The experience you gained from these activities might include the following:

Types of Experience

Work	Experience Gained
Advertising researcher	Helped to develop advertising campaigns; used organizational and time-management skills to complete projects and meet deadlines; worked with copywriters, art directors, and clients; conducted focus group interviews to obtain customer information; compiled and used demographic data.

Nonwork	
Political campaign volunteer	Canvassed neighborhoods; operated a phone bank; helped organize mailings; accomplished tasks on short notice.
Amateur photographer	Learned to use film and video equipment; learned how to develop and print photographs and edit videotapes.

After you've completed this section of your personal inventory, examine it closely to identify any trends or consistencies in the types of experience you have had. Two such consistencies stand out in the example just given. Conducting focus group interviews is a similar experience to canvassing neighborhoods; both involve questioning people to obtain their opinions. Meeting deadlines and accomplishing tasks on short notice also match each other. While you are spotting these consistencies, you should also make note of which types of experience you enjoyed the most and which you disliked.

Education

In going over your educational background, apply the same method you used to inventory your experience. It's important to write out more than the usual two-line listings of schools attended and degrees received. Write down the subject areas you have studied and the specific classes you have taken. Include any seminars or workshops you attended to maintain or improve your skills or to familiarize yourself with a new field.

In our case, for example, we both have MBAs. When the various courses we've taken are compared side by side, however, it becomes apparent that our educational backgrounds are not identical. In addition to the standard management curriculum, Gregory took specialized courses in labor arbitration, transportation systems, and investments and securities. Patricia's studies, on the other hand, included classes in consumer behavior and advertising strategies. Thus, although we hold the same degree, each of us has a different reservoir of knowledge. We can use this knowledge in our consulting practice if we so choose, just as the academic knowledge you have gained can be used in your practice. Naturally, what gets used and what doesn't depends on which consulting field you pick.

Skills

Your experience and education make up two-thirds of your qualifications. The remaining third is composed of your skills: the specific abilities that you can bring to bear in performing your consulting activities. The skills most frequently cited as being necessary for success as a consultant can be broken down into five types: technical, communication, human relations, administrative, and self-motivation skills.

Technical Skills

Technical skills are the abilities that enable you to provide your consulting services: the ability to design buildings, sell products, manage money, train employees, research new markets, increase efficiency, solve problems, and so on. A consultant who knows about the laws and tariffs that apply in importing and exporting goods has technical skills. So does a consultant who is able to design, conduct, and interpret opinion polls. Other types of technical skills include teaching, engineering, writing, computing, operating equipment, programming, cooking, drawing, practicing medicine, organizing, and accounting. Of course, the list doesn't stop here. There are as many types of technical skills as there are types of knowledge and abilities.

Communication Skills

Communication skills are what enable you to express yourself and to understand others so that ideas and information can be shared. Making a phone call, preparing a report, giving a presentation, reading a trade journal, writing a letter, and meeting with a client all require communication skills. The various communication skills used by consultants include speaking, writing, reading, and listening. Combined, they often take up the majority of a consultant's day. Depending on the type of consulting you do, you may use some skills more than others. The one used by all consultants—and generally regarded as the most important—is listening. Only by listening can you determine the full extent of your clients' needs and concerns and whether they are pleased with your services.

Human Relations Skills

Human relations skills can best be defined as the ability to get along with others and to inspire confidence, cooperation, and loyalty. Consultants sometimes make the mistake of thinking that the only thing that counts is their ability to carry out an assignment—their technical skills. Nothing could be farther from the truth. The relationship between a consultant and a client is a fragile one based on trust and the attainment of mutual goals. To maintain the relationship—and the repeat business and client referrals that go with it—

you must be able to establish a rapport with the people you meet. This entails empathizing with their feelings, adjusting to their habits and preferences, and exhibiting a caring attitude.

Administrative Skills

Administrative skills are what keep a consulting practice going. The more adept you are at managing your resources of time, money, people, and property, the more profitable your consulting practice will be. Consultants with poor administrative skills are at a distinct disadvantage when it comes to keeping track of the everyday details of running a business. Although they may be good at performing individual assignments, they overlook or ignore such equally important activities as setting goals, marketing their services, and collecting fees. For your consulting practice to progress beyond the start-up stage and develop into a viable business, you must have administrative skills.

Self-Motivation Skills

Self-motivation skills are what keep you going. Successful consultants are self-starters. They possess the drive (both mental and physical) to accomplish the tasks of their choosing. Rather than waiting for something to happen or expecting someone to tell them what to do, they create their own opportunities. What's more, they derive much of their satisfaction from their work, viewing it as a rewarding activity, rather than just as a means to an end. The major difference between self-motivated people and others is their ability to maintain their enthusiasm and set new challenges for themselves.

SPECIALIST VERSUS GENERALIST

In picking the consulting field that appeals to you the most, you must also decide whether you want to be a specialist or a generalist. Consultants who are specialists make it a point to know as much as possible about a particular subject or industry, such as electronic security systems or the banking industry, and they limit their work to whatever area they choose. Consultants who are generalists prefer to look at the big picture, cultivating knowledge that can be applied in several areas, rather than just one. Management consultants, who provide a variety of services to different types of clients, would fit into this category.

The thing to remember in choosing between becoming a specialist and becoming a generalist is not to define your services too narrowly or too broadly. If you define your services too narrowly, you run the risk of excluding prospective clients who might be able to benefit from your knowledge. On the other hand, if you define your services too broadly, your credibility as an expert will be diminished.

In addition to considering the scope of your knowledge and services, you should also give some thought to which aspect of problem solving you prefer: the diagnosis or the implementation. In other words, would you rather identify a problem or solve it? Generalists, as a rule, spend more time diagnosing problems. Specialists, who usually aren't brought in until after a problem is known, spend more time actually implementing the necessary changes.

TYPES OF CONSULTING FIELDS

The list that follows illustrates the many different types of consulting fields that you can enter. Whether your interests and qualifications are in computers or community relations, interior design or inventory control, new ventures or nutrition, there is likely to be a consulting field that matches them. Far from being complete, this list is just the beginning. As technologies, work situations, lifestyles, and the environment continue to change, additional demands will arise for the advice and information that consultants can provide.

Types of Consulting Fields

Accounting
Acoustics
Advertising
Agriculture
Aircraft and aerospace
Apparel and textiles
Appraisal
Architecture

Banking
Budgeting
Business
Business communications

Career development
Catering
Chemistry
Civil engineering
Communications
Community relations
Computers
Conference planning
Construction
Contest planning
Conventions
Credit and collection
Customer service

Data processing
Direct mail
Drug and alcohol abuse

Ecology
Education
Electrical engineering
Electronics

Employee compensation and benefits
Employee relations
Employee relocations
Employee selection and training
Employee surveys
Employment services
Energy
Engineering
Entertainment
Environmental planning

Fiber optics
Financial planning
Food services
Foreign licensing
Franchising
Fund raising

Geriatrics
Government procurement
Government regulations
Government relations
Graphic design

Hazardous waste
Health care
Heating and air conditioning
Hospitalization insurance
Hotel management
Human resources

Import-export
Industrial operations
In-house publications
Insurance

Interior design
Inventory control
Investigation services
Investment counseling

Labor relations
Landscaping
Law
Leasing
Lie detector testing
Lighting

Management
Manufacturing
Marketing
Marketing research
Materials management
Medicine
Merchandising
Mergers and acquisitions
Minorities

New-product development
New ventures
Nutrition

Office design and layout
Organization behavior
Organization development

Packaging
Personnel
Physical fitness
Plant design and layout
Plant security
Plastics
Politics
Pollution control

Pricing
Printing
Product design
Production management
Property management
Public opinion polls
Public relations
Publishing
Purchasing

Quality control

Real estate
Recreation
Research and development
Retailing
Risk management

Safety engineering
Sales forecasting
Sales management
Sales promotion
Sales training
Salvage and reclamation
Security systems
Shipping and receiving
Small business development
Speech therapy
Strategic planning

Tax planning
Telecommunications
Testing
Time management
Training
Transportation

Urban planning

Utilities management

Venture capital
Video production

Warehousing
Wholesaling
Writing

3

Setting Up Your Business

Possessing the knowledge and expertise to be a consultant is one thing; establishing a practice and running it successfully can be something else. What's needed isn't vast sums of investment capital or a client list a mile long, but something much more basic and essential: a business plan. Before you can help others to achieve their goals, you must first set goals of your own . . . then take the appropriate steps to meet them.

START WITH A PLAN

Having chosen the field or fields in which you want to consult, your first impulse may be to rush out and get business cards printed or pick up the phone and start calling prospective clients. Don't—not without developing a plan of action. Taking the time to answer some key questions in the beginning will save you time (and money) later. For instance, start by asking yourself the following:

- Is my consulting practice going to be a part-time or full-time operation?

- Will clients come to my office, or will I go to theirs?
- Do I want the business based in my home or an outside location?
- What furnishings or equipment do I need?
- What licenses or permits am I required to obtain?
- Which legal form is best for me: a sole proprietorship, partnership, or corporation?
- What kinds of insurance should I have?
- How much should I charge for my services?
- Which individuals or institutions are most likely to want what I have to offer?
- What image do I want to convey?
- How can I maintain good client relations?
- What revenues do I project for the year?

It's important to answer these questions and more at the outset. The resultant business plan you create will help you direct and coordinate the various activities connected with your consulting practice. In addition to this, it gives you the edge when it comes to making the best use of your resources. Instead of going after any and all clients, you can focus on your best prospects. Once you've scheduled a meeting, there's a greater likelihood that an actual consulting assignment will follow.

Some of the issues raised here—such as setting your fees, marketing your services, and meeting with clients—are discussed in separate chapters later in the book. For the moment, though, let's start with the basics: selecting the location for your consulting practice; determining what supplies and equipment you will need; obtaining the necessary licenses, permits, and insurance; and choosing the legal form that is best for you. Once you've addressed the nuts-and-bolts aspects of starting a business, your consulting practice will be several steps closer to opening its doors.

YOUR LOCATION

The location you select for your consulting practice will play an important role in its development, influencing your method of operation, ability to serve clients' needs, and ultimate earnings potential. You should therefore consider each of the following alternatives before deciding which type of office location will work best for you:

- Home-based office
- Convenience office
- Shared office
- Private office

Each has its own advantages and disadvantages, all of which you should bear in mind. Then, based on your budget, working habits, types of clients, and desired image, you can select the location that is most appropriate for your needs.

Home-Based Office

Many beginning consultants—and established ones, too—choose to work out of their homes. One of the main advantages of this choice is the money you can save by not having to rent office space. Rent payments are often the single largest expense in running a business, so your savings can be significant. In addition to lowering your overhead, locating your consulting practice at home makes you eligible for a number of tax deductions. Specifically, it allows you to deduct a part of the operating and depreciation expenses on your home. In other words, a percentage of your mortgage payments or rent, depreciation, property taxes, insurance, utilities, and expenses for household maintenance, repairs, or improvements is deductible. Details on how and when to take advantage of these deductions are discussed in Chapter 14.

Running your consulting practice from your home has other advantages besides financial ones, including the personal freedom to work whenever you choose, rather than adhering to a nine-to-five schedule; increased family togetherness; reduced stress associated with trying to be in two places at once (your home and your office).

On the minus side, however, bear in mind that a home-based office isn't for everyone. First of all, there's the matter of space. You will need to set aside, at the very least, space for office furniture and any supplies or equipment used in your consulting practice. If you're planning to hold meetings with clients at your office, working out of your home may be impractical, depending on your distance from clients and the kind of image you want to project.

There's also your temperament to consider. Some consultants find that they accomplish more if they actually leave the house each day and go to an outside office at a separate location. Separating your work environment from your home environment in this way can stimulate a feeling of professionalism. Finally, you should consider that outside offices generally provide more privacy than home-based offices, thus keeping distractions to a minimum.

Convenience Office

Faced with the choice of working at home or establishing an outside office, a growing number of independent consultants are discovering a middle ground: the convenience office. Sometimes called *executive office suites*, these offices provide consultants and others with working space and a host of amenities that might otherwise be too costly for their budgets. Located in buildings designed especially for convenience offices, each office is a separate unit but has access to a central reception area, conference rooms, and support services such as telephone answering, typing, and photocopying. Other features include fax and accounting services, video equipment, teleconferencing, and on-site travel ticketing. For the consultant who wants the benefits of a private office and a full staff—without the bother of full-time maintenance—this could be the answer.

Beware, however: Convenience comes at a price. Although leasing a convenience office is generally less expensive than setting up an outside office complete with office equipment and full-time secretary, it still isn't cheap. When you add up the total cost of the various services, you may find that you've exceeded your budget. Inasmuch as these services are usually offered on an à la carte basis, it's easy to do. In evaluating convenience offices and determining which, if any, is right for you, make note of each facility's layout and appearance, tenant mix, types of services provided, costs, and administration.

To find out more about convenience offices, you might start by contacting two of the leading companies in this field:

H.Q. Services and Offices
120 Montgomery St.
San Francisco, CA 94104

Omni Offices
3390 Peachtree Rd., N.E.
Atlanta, GA 30326

Both of these companies have convenience office leasing facilities throughout the United States and can provide you with information about what's available in your area.

Shared Office

A simple and effective solution to your office-space needs may be to team up with another consultant and share. Consultants whose practices complement each other—such as an architect and an interior designer, a physical-fitness adviser and a nutritionist, or a management consultant and a marketing specialist—often do this as a matter of course. Not only does a shared office help to keep overhead expenses down, but officemates often prove to be good sources of client referrals. When one consultant is out of the office, having the other on hand is a way to reduce the cost of support services.

For this alternative to work for you, it's essential to find an officemate with whom you are compatible, both professionally and personally. In addition to having similar space requirements for your respective consulting practices, you should agree on how much to spend on rent and furnishings, the kind of image that best suits you, and how clients are to be treated.

If an appropriate officemate doesn't come to mind or you're reluctant to enter into a lease agreement, maybe "desk space" in an existing office would fill the bill. In this instance, you would sublet space in another office that has the extra space available. For example, real estate appraisers frequently set up shop in real estate brokerage or savings and loan offices. The amount of space rented in this situation can range from a desk and chairs with a telephone to a separate office suite with full support services.

Private Office

Leasing and furnishing a private office involves a greater commitment of your resources than the other alternatives discussed, but it also gives you the most control over your environment. Without having to make compromises with family members, building administrators, or officemates, you can set up your consulting practice exactly the way you want it. To save the expense of a secretary, many consultants find that an answering service or automatic answering machine works fine for them. Typing and bookkeeping, particularly when you're just starting out, can probably be handled by a part-time employee or outside service.

If you're thinking of locating your consulting office in a newer building in the heart of the central business district, make sure that your projected revenues justify the expense. Is this, in fact, where your potential clients will be? Is it the best location from which to serve them? Would an office in an older, less expensive building meet your needs and theirs just as well? Would it matter if your office were located outside the central business district? You should try to avoid falling victim to the "mahogany-desk syndrome": spending so much on office space and furnishings that the business itself is put in jeopardy.

SUPPLIES AND EQUIPMENT

Each type of consulting practice has its own unique requirements for supplies and equipment. For example, a career guidance consultant needs to maintain a reference library on the present and future state of the job market. Along with this, video equipment may be required to make tape recordings of clients in simulated job in- terviews. A product designer, on the other hand, has different needs: a drafting table, drawing supplies, and a computer with graphic design capabilities.

While your consulting practice is still in the early stages, there's no need to purchase all your supplies and equipment at once. In- stead, make a list of the essentials you will need to perform your initial consulting assignments. Then obtain these items—stationery, work materials, office equipment, furniture, and fixtures—as eco- nomically as possible. To get your money's worth, be sure to com- pare the pros and cons of leasing versus buying furnishings and equipment.

By using some ingenuity, you can get the things you need and still stay within your budget. For instance, office furnishings can often be bought at public auctions. Stationery and other supplies can be purchased at discount office supply stores. With the prices of computer hardware and software, fax machines, copiers, cellular phones, and other electronic equipment coming down, a high-tech office doesn't have to carry a high price tag.

LICENSES, PERMITS, AND INSURANCE

To keep your consulting practice legal and to protect yourself against liabilities, it's important to obtain any licenses or permits that are required, along with adequate insurance coverage. What you need depends on the nature of your consulting practice and where it's located. The following information should help you make the ap- propriate decisions in this area. As an added measure of protection, you should also confer with an attorney or insurance agent.

Business Tax and Permit

To operate your consulting practice, you may need to pay a busi- ness tax and obtain a permit, commonly known as a business *li- cense*. This is usually issued by the city and/or county in which a business is located and is valid for one to two years. The fee can range from less than $50 to several hundred dollars. To find out if consulting practices located in your area are required to have a business license, contact the office of the city clerk in your municipality.

Occupational License

To maintain set standards of performance and guard the safety of consumers, most states regulate entry into certain consulting fields, such as health services, engineering, and accounting. If you will be consulting in a regulated field, you must first meet the standards set forth by the state licensing board governing your occupation. Once you have demonstrated your competence, you will be issued a license. Most licenses are valid for a period of one to two years, at which time they are renewable. To determine if an occupational license is required for your consulting field, check with your state's department of consumer affairs.

Fictitious Business Name Statement

If your consulting firm's name is different from your own name (e.g., Creative Consultants; The Nutrition Specialists), then you will probably have to file a fictitious business name statement with the county clerk's office. The purpose of this statement is to make available to the public your identity and the identities of any others who are co-workers of your consulting firm. As a rule of thumb, a fictitious name statement is required in the following situations:

- When the surnames of all owners are not included in the consulting firm's name
- When the existence of additional owners is suggested by the consulting firm's name (e.g., Jones and Associates; The Abbott Consulting Group; Campbell and Company)
- When the name of the consulting firm (if it is a corporation) is not included in its articles of incorporation

Consultants who are active in more than one field or who want to spin off separate businesses from their consulting practices can file more than one fictitious business name. In our case, for instance, we have the following fictitious business names: K & K Enterprises, Kishel Consulting Group, The Business Builders, and American Business Press.

The time to file a fictitious name statement (Figure 3-1) is within 40 days after your consulting practice commences operations. This process involves (1) filing the statement with the county clerk and (2) having the statement published in a newspaper of general circulation. The second part is to ensure that the public has an opportunity to see your statement. To save time and simplify the process, instead of going to the county clerk's office first, go directly to the newspaper where your statement will appear. Most newspapers carry fictitious name forms as a convenience to their customers and will not only file the completed statement for you, but will also assist you in filling it out. The total cost for filing and publishing the statement should be somewhere between $25 and $75.

Employer Identification Number

If you employ one or more people in your consulting practice, the federal government requires you to have an employer identification number. This enables the government to verify that you are paying all appropriate employer taxes and withholding the proper amounts from employee paychecks. Even if your consulting practice is a one-person operation without any employees, it's still advisable to obtain an identification number, primarily because clients often need it for their records. If you should decide to hire someone later, take in a partner, or incorporate your business, you will need the number for tax purposes.

It's an easy matter to get an employer identification number for your consulting practice. What's more, there is no fee for it. To obtain one, all you need to do is fill out IRS Form SS-4 (Figure 3-2) and submit it to the Internal Revenue Service.

Figure 3-1   Fictitious Business Name Statement

A	MAIL FILED DOCUMENTS TO:		COUNTY CLERK'S FILING STAMP
NAME			
ADDRESS			
CITY/STATE/ZIP			
DAYTIME PHONE ( )			

1	❏ First Filing ❏ Renewal Filing ❏ With Changes Current Registration No _____	B	PUBLISH IN NEWSPAPER:

FICTITIOUS BUSINESS NAME STATEMENT
THE FOLLOWING PERSON(S) IS (ARE) DOING BUSINESS AS:

2	Fictitious Business Name(s) 1. 2.	3. Articles of Incorporation Number (If applicable) AI #
3	Street Address, City & State of Principal Place of Business in California	Zip Code

4	Full name of Registrant	(If corporation - show state of incorporation)		
	Residence Street Address	City	State	Zip Code

4A	Full name of Registrant	(If corporation - show state of incorporation)		
	Residence Street Address	City	State	Zip Code

4B	Full name of Registrant	(If corporation - show state of incorporation)		
	Residence Street Address	City	State	Zip Code

5	This Business is Conducted by (check only one)	❏ an individual ❏ husband & wife ❏ a general partnership ❏ a limited partnership ❏ a corporation ❏ a business trust ❏ co-partners ❏ joint venture ❏ an unincorporated association other than a partnership ❏ other (please specify) _____

6	Type of Business: Examples: Auto Repairing, Leasing, Beauty Salon, Landscaping

7	❏ The registrant commenced to transact business under the fictitious name or names listed above on (Date): _____ ❏ Registrant has not yet begun to transact business under the fictitious business name or names listed herein.

8	If Registrant is not a corporation sign below:		8A	If Registrant is a corporation sign below:
	SIGNATURE TYPE OR PRINT NAME			CORPORATION NAME
	SIGNATURE TYPE OR PRINT NAME			SIGNATURE & TITLE
	SIGNATURE TYPE OR PRINT NAME			TYPE OR PRINT NAME AND TITLE

9	This statement was filed with the County Clerk of _____ County on date indicated by file stamp above. File Number: _____

NOTICE — THIS FICTITIOUS NAME STATEMENT EXPIRES FIVE YEARS FROM THE DATE IT WAS FILED IN THE OFFICE OF THE COUNTY CLERK. A NEW FICTITIOUS BUSINESS NAME STATEMENT MUST BE FILED PRIOR TO THAT DATE. The filing of this statement does not of itself authorize the use in this state of a fictitious business name in violation of the rights of another under federal, state, or common law (See Section 14400 et seq., Business and Professions Code.)

PLEASE PRINT OR TYPE   SEE REVERSE SIDE FOR INSTRUCTIONS
(rev. 1/94)
California Newspaper Service Bureau

Figure 3-2   Application for Employer Identification Number (IRS Form SS-4)

Form **SS-4** (Rev. December 1993) Department of the Treasury Internal Revenue Service	**Application for Employer Identification Number** (For use by employers, corporations, partnerships, trusts, estates, churches, government agencies, certain individuals, and others. See instructions.)	EIN OMB No. 1545-0003 Expires 12-31-96

Please type or print clearly.

1 Name of applicant (Legal name) (See instructions.)

2 Trade name of business, if different from name in line 1	**3** Executor, trustee, "care of" name
4a Mailing address (street address) (room, apt., or suite no.)	**5a** Business address, if different from address in lines 4a and 4b
4b City, state, and ZIP code	**5b** City, state, and ZIP code

6 County and state where principal business is located

7 Name of principal officer, general partner, grantor, owner, or trustor—SSN required (See instructions.) ▶

8a Type of entity (Check only one box.) (See instructions.)
☐ Sole Proprietor (SSN) _____
☐ REMIC   ☐ Personal service corp.
☐ State/local government   ☐ National guard
☐ Other nonprofit organization (specify) _____
☐ Other (specify) ▶ _____

☐ Estate (SSN of decedent) _____
☐ Plan administrator-SSN _____
☐ Other corporation (specify) _____
☐ Federal government/military   ☐ Church or church controlled organization
_____ (enter GEN if applicable) _____

☐ Trust
☐ Partnership
☐ Farmers' cooperative

8b If a corporation, name the state or foreign country (if applicable) where incorporated ▶

State	Foreign country

9 Reason for applying (Check only one box.)
☐ Started new business (specify) ▶ _____
☐ Hired employees
☐ Created a pension plan (specify type) ▶ _____
☐ Banking purpose (specify) ▶ _____

☐ Changed type of organization (specify) ▶ _____
☐ Purchased going business
☐ Created a trust (specify) ▶ _____
☐ Other (specify) ▶

10 Date business started or acquired (Mo., day, year) (See instructions.)	**11** Enter closing month of accounting year. (See instructions.)

12 First date wages or annuities were paid or will be paid (Mo., day, year). **Note:** *If applicant is a withholding agent, enter date income will first be paid to nonresident alien. (Mo., day, year)* . . . . ▶

13 Enter highest number of employees expected in the next 12 months. **Note:** *If the applicant does not expect to have any employees during the period, enter "0."* . . . . ▶	Nonagricultural	Agricultural	Household

14 Principal activity (See instructions.) ▶

15 Is the principal business activity manufacturing? . . . . ☐ **Yes**   ☐ **No**
If "Yes," principal product and raw material used ▶

16 To whom are most of the products or services sold? Please check the appropriate box.   ☐ Business (wholesale)
☐ Public (retail)   ☐ Other (specify) ▶   ☐ N/A

17a Has the applicant ever applied for an identification number for this or any other business? . . . . ☐ **Yes**   ☐ **No**
Note: *If "Yes," please complete lines 17b and 17c.*

17b If you checked the "Yes" box in line 17a, give applicant's legal name and trade name, if different than name shown on prior application.

Legal name ▶   Trade name ▶

17c Enter approximate date, city, and state where the application was filed and the previous employer identification number if known.

Approximate date when filed (Mo., day, year)	City and state where filed	Previous EIN

Under penalties of perjury, I declare that I have examined this application, and to the best of my knowledge and belief, it is true, correct, and complete.	Business telephone number (include area code)

Name and title (Please type or print clearly.) ▶

Signature ▶   Date ▶

Note: *Do not write below this line.   For official use only.*

Please leave blank ▶	Geo.	Ind.	Class	Size	Reason for applying

For Paperwork Reduction Act Notice, see attached instructions.   Cat. No. 16055N   Form **SS-4** (Rev. 12-93)

Seller's Permit

In obtaining the various licenses and permits you need to operate your consulting practice, you should also investigate the possibility of getting a seller's permit. If you plan to sell products in addition to providing consulting services and your state taxes retail sales, then you will need a seller's permit. For instance, consultants who market their information via audiocassettes, newsletters, and books are likely to need seller's permits. So are interior designers who sell furniture and accessories to their clients, and nutritionists who sell vitamins.

A seller's permit (1) exempts you from paying sales tax on the merchandise you purchase from suppliers to resell through your consulting firm and (2) authorizes you to collect the sales tax from your clients. In addition, a seller's permit enables you to gain entry to product trade shows and to purchase goods at wholesale prices.

Although there is no fee for a seller's permit, you may be required to post a bond, depending on your estimated gross sales of taxable merchandise. This bond is to ensure that you collect and remit to the state all sales tax due. To find out more about the seller's permit and whether you need one, check with your state's tax board.

Trademark, Copyrights, and Patents

As an independent consultant, your main stock-in-trade is knowledge. To protect your ideas and inventions, you should be aware of the purposes and uses of trademarks, copyrights, and patents.

Trademarks

Consultants, perhaps even more than other entrepreneurs, depend on customer loyalty and referrals to generate sales. Creating a recognizable name for your consulting firm is one way to increase your visibility and build up your practice. Having created such a name, though, you want to make sure that you derive the full benefits from it. This can frequently be accomplished by registering the name as your business's trademark. To do this, you must file a Trademark/ Service Mark Application form with the U.S. Department of Commerce (Figure 3-3).

By definition, a trademark is any word, name, symbol, device, or combination of these used to identify the products or services of a business and to distinguish them from those of other enterprises. To qualify as a registerable trademark, your name or symbol must not be confusingly similar to any existing trademarks of consulting firms in your field. Ideally, it should have positive connotations and be distinctive and easy to pronounce. Note that you cannot trademark your surname as the name of your consulting firm or products because others with the same last name would be free to use it, too. However, if you create a distinctive logotype that incorporates your name or initials into the graphic design, *that* can be trademarked.

Once granted, a trademark is good for ten years and may be renewed indefinitely. Although you are not legally required to register your trademark at all, it is definitely advisable to do so, inasmuch as this gives you the greatest protection. You can find out more about how and when to use a trademark by writing to the U.S. Department of Commerce, Patent and Trademark Office, Washington DC 20231. Ask them to send you their pamphlet "General Information Concerning Trademarks."

Copyrights

In addition to safeguarding your business name, you can also safeguard your creations. One of the tools that enables you to do this is the copyright. Although most commonly associated with literary works, copyright protection extends to graphic designs, paintings, sculpture, musical compositions, sound recordings, and audiovisual works. Given this broad coverage, many consultants can benefit from copyright protection. A sampling of works that come within the scope of copyright coverage includes reports, charts, technical drawings, graphic designs, computer programs, advertising copy, photographs, catalogs, brochures, newsletters, books, audiocassettes, and video recordings.

Figure 3-3   Trademark/Service Mark Application

TRADEMARK/SERVICE MARK APPLICATION, PRINCIPAL REGISTER, WITH DECLARATION	MARK (Word(s) and/or Design)	CLASS NO. (If known)

TO THE ASSISTANT COMMISSIONER FOR TRADEMARKS:

APPLICANT'S NAME:

APPLICANT'S BUSINESS ADDRESS:
(Display address exactly as it should appear on registration)

APPLICANT'S ENTITY TYPE: (Check one and supply requested information)

Individual - Citizen of (Country):

Partnership - State where organized (Country, if appropriate):
Names and Citizenship (Country) of General Partners: _____

Corporation - State (Country, if appropriate) of Incorporation:

Other (Specific Nature of Entity and Domicile):

GOODS AND/OR SERVICES:

Applicant requests registration of the trademark/service mark shown in the accompanying drawing in the United States Patent and Trademark Office on the Principal Register established by the Act of July 5, 1946 (15 U.S.C. 1051 et. seq., as amended) for the following goods/services (**SPECIFIC GOODS AND/OR SERVICES MUST BE INSERTED HERE**):

BASIS FOR APPLICATION: (Check boxes which apply, but never both the first AND second boxes, and supply requested information related to each box checked.)

[ ] Applicant is using mark in commerce on or in connection with the above identified goods/services. (15 U.S.C. 1051(a), as amended.) Three specimens showing the mark as used in commerce are submitted with this application.
  ● Date of first use of the mark in commerce which the U.S. Congress may regulate (for example, interstate or between the U.S. and a foreign country): _____
  ● Specify the type of commerce: _____
    (for example, interstate or between the U.S. and a specified foreign country)
  ● Date of first use anywhere (the same as or before use in commerce date): _____
  ● Specify intended manner or mode of use of mark on or in connection with the goods/services: _____
    (for example, trademark is applied to labels, service mark is used in advertisements)

[ ] Applicant has a bona fide intention to use the mark in commerce on or in connection with the above identified goods/services. (15 U.S.C. 1051(b), as amended.)
  ● Specify manner or mode of use of mark on or in connection with the goods/services: _____
    (for example, trademark will be applied to labels, service mark will be used in advertisements)

[ ] Applicant has a bona fide intention to use the mark in commerce on or in connection with the above identified goods/services and asserts a claim of priority based upon a foreign application in accordance with 15 U.S.C. 1126(d), as amended.
  ● Country of foreign filing: _____   ● Date of foreign filing: _____

[ ] Applicant has a bona fide intention to use the mark in commerce or in connection with the above identified goods/services, and, accompanying this application, submits a certification or certified copy of a foreign registration in accordance with 15 U.S.C 1126(e), as amended.
  ● Country of registration: _____   ● Registration number: _____

NOTE: Declaration, on Reverse Side, MUST be Signed

PTO Form 1478 (REV 10/94)   U.S. DEPARTMENT OF COMMERCE/Patent and Trademark Office
OMB No. 0651-0009 (Exp. 6/30/95)

Figure 3-3   *(Continued)*

If submitted on one page, side two of the form should be Upside Down" in relation to page 1.

DECLARATION

The undersigned being hereby warned that willful false statements and the like so made are punishable by fine or imprisonment, or both, under 18 U.S.C. 1001, and that such willful false statements may jeopardize the validity of the application or any resulting registration, declares that he/she is properly authorized to execute this application this application on behalf of the applicant; he/she believes the applicant to be owner of the trademark/service mark sought to be registered, or if the application is being files under 15 U.S.C. 1051(b), he/she believes applicant to be entitled to use such mark in commerce; to the best of his/her knowledge and belief no other person, firm, corporation, or association has the right to use the above identified mark in commerce, either in the identical form thereof or in such near resemblance thereto as to be likely, when used on or in connection with the goods/services of such other person, to cause confusion, or to cause mistake, or to deceive; and that all statements made of his/her own knowledge are true and that all statements made on information and belief are believed to be true.

DATE   SIGNATURE

TELEPHONE NUMBER   PRINT OR TYPE NAME

INSTRUCTIONS AND INFORMATION FOR APPLICANT

TO RECEIVE A FILING DATE, THE APPLICATION MUST BE COMPLETED AND SIGNED BY THE APPLICANT AND SUBMITTED ALONG WITH:

1. The prescribed **FEE of $245.00*** for each class of goods/services listed in the application;
2. A **DRAWING PAGE** displaying the mark in conformance with 37 CFR 2.52;
3. If the application is based on use of the mark in commerce, **THREE (3) SPECIMENS** (evidence) of the mark as used in commerce for each class of goods/services listed in the application. All three specimens may be in the nature of: (a) labels showing the mark which are placed on the goods; (b) photographs of the mark as it appears on the goods, (c) brochures or advertisements showing the mark as used in connection with the services.
4. An **APPLICATION WITH DECLARATION** (this form) - The application must be signed in order for the application to receive a filing date. Only the following person may sign the declaration, depending on the applicant's legal entity: (a) the individual applicant; (b) an officer of the corporate applicant; (c) one general partner of a partnership applicant; (d) all joint applicants.

SEND APPLICATION FORM, DRAWING PAGE, FEE AND SPECIMENS (IF APPROPRIATE) TO:

Assistant Commissioner for Trademarks
Box New App / Fee
2900 Crystal Drive
Arlington, VA 22202-3513

Additional information concerning the requirements for filing an application is available in a booklet entitled **Basic Facts About Registering a Trademark,** which may be obtained by writing to the above address or by calling: (703) 308-9000.

* Fees are subject to change; changes usually take effect on October 1. If filing on or after October 1, 1995, please call the PTO to confirm the correct fee.

This form is estimated to take an average of 1 hour to complete, including time required for reading and understanding instructions, gathering necessary information, recordkeeping, and actually providing the information. Any comments on this form, including the amount of time required to complete this form, should be sent to the Office of Management and Organizations, U.S. Patent and Trademark Office, U.S. Department of Commerce, Washington, D.C. 20231, and Paper Reduction Project 0651-0009, Office of Information and Regulatory Affairs, Office of Management and Budget, Washington, D.C. 20503. Do NOT send completed forms to either of these addresses.

Copyrighting any of your creations is relatively simple. All you need to do is provide public notice of the copyright on the work itself and file an application for copyright registration. The fee for this is $20 and you should be able to complete the paperwork by yourself. Once granted, a copyright is valid for up to 50 years after the holder's death. For more information on copyrights, write to the Copyright Office, Library of Congress, Washington, DC 20559. Make sure to specify the type of work you would like to copyright so that you receive the appropriate information and registration form. A sample copyright form is shown in Figure 3-4.

Patents

The other major tool that enables you to safeguard your creations is the patent. If, in the course of carrying out your consulting activities, you develop a product, process, or design that you believe has commercial possibilities, obtaining a patent may be advisable. In granting a patent to an inventor, the federal government gives him or her the right to exclude all others from making, using, or selling the patented invention in the United States. Design patents, covering only the style or appearance of a product, are granted for periods of three and a half, seven, or 14 years, as specified in the patent application. Patents for new and useful products or processes are valid for 20 years from the day of application.

Obtaining a patent is considerably more involved than applying for a trademark or copyright. The federal government advises inventors to seek out the help of an attorney or agent skilled in preparing patent applications. The total cost, including the government's filing and issuing fees, is usually between $1,500 and $5,000. Given the potentially high stakes involved if your invention is indeed a winner, proceed with caution. It's important to be informed each step of the way throughout the patent-application process. To get the basic facts on obtaining a patent, write to the U.S. Department of Commerce, Patent and Trademark Office, Washington, DC 20231. Ask them to send you their pamphlet "Patents and Inventions: An Information Aid for Inventors."

Figure 3-4   Copyright Registration Application (Form TX)

FORM TX
For a Literary Work
UNITED STATES COPYRIGHT OFFICE

REGISTRATION NUMBER

TX   TXU

EFFECTIVE DATE OF REGISTRATION

Month   Day   Year

DO NOT WRITE ABOVE THIS LINE. IF YOU NEED MORE SPACE, USE A SEPARATE CONTINUATION SHEET.

1

TITLE OF THIS WORK ▼

PREVIOUS OR ALTERNATIVE TITLES ▼

PUBLICATION AS A CONTRIBUTION If this work was published as a contribution to a periodical, serial, or collection, give information about the collective work in which the contribution appeared.   **Title of Collective Work ▼**

If published in a periodical or serial give: Volume ▼   Number ▼   Issue Date ▼   On Pages ▼

2 **a**

NAME OF AUTHOR ▼

DATES OF BIRTH AND DEATH
Year Born ▼   Year Died ▼

Was this contribution to the work a "work made for hire"?
☐ Yes
☐ No

AUTHOR'S NATIONALITY OR DOMICILE
Name of Country
OR { Citizen of ▶
     { Domiciled in▶

WAS THIS AUTHOR'S CONTRIBUTION TO THE WORK
Anonymous?   ☐ Yes ☐ No
Pseudonymous? ☐ Yes ☐ No
If the answer to either of these questions is "Yes," see detailed instructions.

NATURE OF AUTHORSHIP Briefly describe nature of material created by this author in which copyright is claimed. ▼

NOTE

Under the law, the "author" of a "work made for hire" is generally the employer, not the employee (see instructions). For any part of this work that was "made for hire" check "Yes" in the space provided, give the employer (or other person for whom the work was prepared) as "Author" of that part, and leave the space for dates of birth and death blank.

b

NAME OF AUTHOR ▼

DATES OF BIRTH AND DEATH
Year Born ▼   Year Died ▼

Was this contribution to the work a "work made for hire"?
☐ Yes
☐ No

AUTHOR'S NATIONALITY OR DOMICILE
Name of Country
OR { Citizen of ▶
     { Domiciled in▶

WAS THIS AUTHOR'S CONTRIBUTION TO THE WORK
Anonymous?   ☐ Yes ☐ No
Pseudonymous? ☐ Yes ☐ No
If the answer to either of these questions is "Yes," see detailed instructions.

NATURE OF AUTHORSHIP Briefly describe nature of material created by this author in which copyright is claimed. ▼

c

NAME OF AUTHOR ▼

DATES OF BIRTH AND DEATH
Year Born ▼   Year Died ▼

Was this contribution to the work a "work made for hire"?
☐ Yes
☐ No

AUTHOR'S NATIONALITY OR DOMICILE
Name of Country
OR { Citizen of ▶
     { Domiciled in▶

WAS THIS AUTHOR'S CONTRIBUTION TO THE WORK
Anonymous?   ☐ Yes ☐ No
Pseudonymous? ☐ Yes ☐ No
If the answer to either of these questions is "Yes," see detailed instructions.

NATURE OF AUTHORSHIP Briefly describe nature of material created by this author in which copyright is claimed. ▼

3 **a**

YEAR IN WHICH CREATION OF THIS WORK WAS COMPLETED This information must be given
◀ Year in all cases.

DATE AND NATION OF FIRST PUBLICATION OF THIS PARTICULAR WORK
Complete this information   Month ▶   Day ▶   Year ▶
ONLY if this work has been published.
◀ Nation

4

COPYRIGHT CLAIMANT(S) Name and address must be given even if the claimant is the same as the author given in space 2. ▼

See instructions before completing this space.

TRANSFER If the claimant(s) named here in space 4 is (are) different from the author(s) named in space 2, give a brief statement of how the claimant(s) obtained ownership of the copyright. ▼

APPLICATION RECEIVED

ONE DEPOSIT RECEIVED

TWO DEPOSITS RECEIVED

FUNDS RECEIVED

DO NOT WRITE HERE
OFFICE USE ONLY

MORE ON BACK ▶ • Complete all applicable spaces (numbers 5-11) on the reverse side of this page.
• See detailed instructions.   • Sign the form at line 10.

DO NOT WRITE HERE

Page 1 of   pages

Figure 3-4   *(Continued)*

EXAMINED BY	FORM TX
CHECKED BY	
☐ CORRESPONDENCE Yes	FOR COPYRIGHT OFFICE USE ONLY

DO NOT WRITE ABOVE THIS LINE. IF YOU NEED MORE SPACE, USE A SEPARATE CONTINUATION SHEET.

PREVIOUS REGISTRATION Has registration for this work, or for an earlier version of this work, already been made in the Copyright Office?

☐ **Yes** ☐ **No** If your answer is "Yes," why is another registration being sought? (Check appropriate box) ▼

a. ☐ This is the first published edition of a work previously registered in unpublished form.

b. ☐ This is the first application submitted by this author as copyright claimant.

c. ☐ This is a changed version of the work, as shown by space 6 on this application.

If your answer is "Yes," give: **Previous Registration Number** ▼   **Year of Registration** ▼

5

DERIVATIVE WORK OR COMPILATION Complete both space 6a and 6b for a derivative work; complete only 6b for a compilation.

a. Preexisting Material Identify any preexisting work or works that this work is based on or incorporates. ▼

b. Material Added to This Work Give a brief, general statement of the material that has been added to this work and in which copyright is claimed. ▼

See instructions
before completing
this space.

6

—space deleted—

7

REPRODUCTION FOR USE OF BLIND OR PHYSICALLY HANDICAPPED INDIVIDUALS A signature on this form at space 10 and a check in one of the boxes here in space 8 constitutes a non-exclusive grant of permission to the Library of Congress to reproduce and distribute solely for the blind and physically handicapped and under the conditions and limitations prescribed by the regulations of the Copyright Office: (1) copies of the work identified in space 1 of this application in Braille (or similar tactile symbols); or (2) phonorecords embodying a fixation of a reading of that work; or (3) both.

a ☐ Copies and Phonorecords   b ☐ Copies Only   c ☐ Phonorecords Only

See instructions.

8

DEPOSIT ACCOUNT If the registration fee is to be charged to a Deposit Account established in the Copyright Office, give name and number of Account.

Name ▼   **Account Number** ▼

CORRESPONDENCE Give name and address to which correspondence about this application should be sent.   Name/Address/Apt/City/State/ZIP ▼

Area Code and Telephone Number ▶

Be sure to
give your
daytime phone
◀ number.

9

CERTIFICATION* I, the undersigned, hereby certify that I am the

Check only one ▶
☐ author
☐ other copyright claimant
☐ owner of exclusive right(s)
☐ authorized agent of

of the work identified in this application and that the statements made
by me in this application are correct to the best of my knowledge.

Name of author or other copyright claimant, or owner of exclusive right(s) ▲

Typed or printed name and date ▼ If this application gives a date of publication in space 3, do not sign and submit it before that date.

date ▶

👉 **Handwritten signature (X)** ▼

10

MAIL CERTIFI- CATE TO	Name ▼	YOU MUST: • Complete all necessary spaces • Sign your application in space 10
	Number/Street/Apartment Number ▼	SEND ALL 3 ELEMENTS IN THE SAME PACKAGE: 1. Application form 2. Nonrefundable $20 filing fee in check or money order payable to *Register of Copyrights* 3. Deposit material
Certificate will be mailed in window envelope	City/State/ZIP ▼	MAIL TO: Register of Copyrights Library of Congress Washington, D.C. 20559-6000

The Copyright Office
has the authority to ad-
just fees at 5-year intervals, based on changes
in the Consumer Price
Index. The next adjust-
ment is due in 1996.
Please contact the
Copyright Office after
July 1995 to determine
the actual fee schedule.

11

*17 U.S.C. § 506(e): Any person who knowingly makes a false representation of a material fact in the application for copyright registration provided for by section 409, or in any written statement filed in connection with the application, shall be fined not more than $2,500.

July 1993—400,000   ♲ PRINTED ON RECYCLED PAPER   ☆U.S. GOVERNMENT PRINTING OFFICE: 1993-342-582/80,020

Insurance

There is no point in setting up your consulting practice if you don't take adequate measures to protect it. In addition to protecting your ideas and inventions, it's important to protect yourself and your practice against financial losses due to accident, illness, professional liability, or theft. Your insurance needs will be determined largely by the type of consulting work you do, where your practice is located, and how your operation is run. The following information should give you an idea of the kinds of insurance that are available.

Fire Insurance

Fire insurance protects your building and the property contained within it against damage inflicted by fire or lightning. Standard fire insurance policies do not cover accounting records, securities, deeds, money, bills, or manuscripts. Nor do they protect you against smoke and water damage that occurs as a result of a fire. To guard excluded valuables and protect against these exempted hazards, additional coverage is needed.

If your consulting practice is located in your home and you already have insurance, your existing policy may provide sufficient protection. Be sure to talk to your insurance agent to determine whether additional coverage is required. Standard homeowner's policies frequently exclude home-space businesses. In the case of convenience office and desk space arrangements, fire insurance may be provided by the lessor. Check your lease agreement to verify this.

Automobile Insurance

If one or more automobiles or trucks will be used in your consulting practice, automobile insurance is a must. It protects you against property damage and bodily-injury claims as well as the actions of uninsured motorists.

The amount of coverage you need and the cost of the policy depend on the number of cars or trucks being insured, their value, the kinds of driving that they'll be used for (driving clients around, transporting materials and equipment), and your location.

Professional Liability Insurance

Any professional who provides advice or information to others or performs a service should seriously consider obtaining professional liability insurance. This protects consultants against damage claims resulting from mistakes they might make or their failure to complete an assignment. The most common type of professional liability insurance for consultants is "errors and omissions insurance." Although the premium can be steep, you may be able to obtain it at a reduced rate by purchasing it through a professional group or association to which you belong.

Personal Insurance

Personal insurance protects both you and your employees, if any, against personal loss. Health and life insurance, a retirement plan, and key personnel insurance all contribute to this protection. Key personnel insurance is particularly important if your consulting firm is a partnership or relies on the services of a key employee. In the event that the key person dies or is disabled, the proceeds from the policy are paid directly to the consulting firm.

Worker's Compensation

Employers are required by law to have worker's compensation insurance for their employees to cover damages arising from on-the-job injuries or occupational diseases. If you intend to employ others in your consulting practice, you will need to obtain this insurance.

Crime Insurance

To protect your property against theft, you'll need some kind of crime insurance. The most popular form is the comprehensive insurance policy. A sort of all-in-one policy, this protects you against not only burglaries and robberies, but a variety of other hazards, as well.

CHOOSING A LEGAL FORM

Last but not least, in setting up your consulting practice, you'll want to choose the legal form that best suits your needs. The three types from which to choose are the sole proprietorship, the partnership, and the corporation. Figure 3-5 sums up the advantages and disadvantages of each form of ownership.

Sole Proprietorship

A consulting practice owned by one person, who is entitled to all of its profits and is responsible for all of its debts, is considered a sole proprietorship. Providing maximum control and minimum government interference, this legal form is currently used by more than 75 percent of all businesses. The main advantages of the sole proprietorship are (1) the ease with which it can be started, (2) the owner's freedom to make decisions, and (3) the distribution of profits (owner takes all).

The sole proprietorship isn't without its disadvantages, though, the most serious of which is its unlimited liability. As a sole proprietor, you are responsible for all business debts. Should these exceed the assets of your consulting firm, your creditors can then claim your personal assets, as well. Sole proprietorships also tend to have more difficulty obtaining capital and retaining key employees. Any consultant who chooses to set up a sole proprietorship should be prepared to work independently, primarily drawing on his or her own resources.

Figure 3-5 Comparison of Different Forms of Ownership

The Advantages and Disadvantages of Each Legal Form of Ownership

Sole Proprietorship

Advantages	Disadvanages
1. You're the boss.	1. You have unlimited liability.
2. It's easy to get the business started.	2. The investment capital you can raise is limited.
3. You keep all the profits.	3. You need to be a generalist.
4. Income from business is taxed as personal income.	4. Retaining high-caliber employees is difficult.
5. You can discontinue your business at will.	5. The life of the business is limited.

Partnership

Advantages	Disadvanages
1. Two heads are better than one.	1. Partners have unlimited liability.
2. It's easy to get started.	2. Profits must be shared.
3. More investment capital is available.	3. The partners may disagree on how to run the business.
4. Partners pay only personal income tax.	4. The life of the business is limited.
5. High-caliber employees can be made partners.	

Corporation

Advantages	Disadvanages
1. Stockholders have limited liability.	1. Corporations are taxed twice.
2. Corporations can raise the most investment capital.	2. Corporations must pay capital stock tax.
3. The business has unlimited life.	3. Starting a corporation is expensive.
4. Ownership is easily transferrable.	4. Corporations are more closely regulated.
5. Corporations can utilize specialists.	

Partnership

A consulting practice owned by two or more people, who agree to share its profits, is considered a partnership. Like the sole proprietorship, a partnership is easy to start, and the red tape involved is usually minimal. The main advantages of a partnership are that the consulting firm can (1) draw on the skills and abilities of each partner, (2) offer employees the chance to become partners, and (3) utilize the partner's combined financial resources.

Partnerships have their share of disadvantages, however. The unlimited liability that applies to sole proprietorships is even worse for partnerships. As a partner in a consulting firm, you are responsible not only for your own business debts, but also for those of your partners. Should your partners incur debts or legal judgments against the consulting practice, you could be held legally responsible for them. Disputes among partners can also be a problem. Before entering into a partnership agreement, make sure that you and your partners see eye to eye on how the consulting practice should be run. (*Note*: For your own protection, you should have a *written* partnership agreement.)

Corporation

A corporation differs from the other legal forms of business in that the law regards it as an artificial being possessing the same rights and responsibilities as a person. Thus, unlike a sole proprietorship or a partnership, it has an existence separate from its owners. As a result, the corporation offers some unique advantages. These include (1) limited liability (owners are not personally responsible for the debts of the business), (2) the option of raising capital by selling shares of stock, and (3) easy transfer of ownership from one individual to another. In addition, again unlike the sole proprietorship and the partnership, the corporation has "unlimited life" and thus the potential to outlive its original owners.

The main disadvantages of the corporation can be summed up in two words: *taxation* and *complexity*. In what amounts to double taxation, you must pay taxes on both the income the corporation earns and the income (salary and dividends) you receive from the corporation. In addition, corporations are required to pay an annual tax on all outstanding shares of stock. Given its complexity, a corporation is both more difficult and more expensive to start than the other legal forms. You must obtain a charter from the state in which your consulting firm is located; this process usually requires the services of an attorney. The total cost of incorporating, including government and attorney fees, generally ranges from $500 to $3,000.

One way to have the advantages of a corporation without its tax disadvantages is to form an *S corporation*. This is a special type of corporation that the IRS taxes as a partnership rather than a corporation. To qualify for S corporation status, your consulting firm must meet the specific requirements set forth by the IRS.

4

Determining Your Consulting Fees

One of the most difficult decisions for new consultants is deciding what price to put on their services. If you set your fees too high, you run the risk of losing potential clients. If you set them too low, you will lose potential profits. Thus, in determining your fees, you want to arrive at a price that is satisfactory to both you and your clients.

COMPUTING YOUR FEES

To compute your consulting fees accurately, you must have a thorough understanding of your needs and those of the marketplace. The fee schedule that you ultimately decide on should take into consideration five major factors: salary, overhead, profit, competition, and the economy.

Salary

The starting point in computing your consulting fees is your salary. In essence, your fees need to be sufficient to provide you with a salary equal to or better than what you could receive by working as an employee in someone else's business. What that salary will be depends partly on your own expectations and personal valuation of your worth to clients. It also depends on the current demand for your services. Highly skilled consultants in high-demand fields can and do command top fees that translate into top salaries. Equally skilled consultants in fields where there is less demand earn proportionally less because of the downward pressure on fees. On the plus side, consultants with relatively little experience—such as recent graduates—can often increase their earning power by focusing on high-demand fields.

If you are uncertain about what your salary should be, check with other consultants in your field to determine an appropriate salary range, or check with the appropriate professional association: Most keep annual statistics on the salary levels of their members. To find out which associations represent your consulting field, refer to the section, "Trade and Professional Associations," in Chapter 15.

Overhead

Overhead is usually defined as the ongoing costs of running a business. It includes, among other things, rent, utilities, telephone, insurance, pension, promotion, typing, photocopying, and travel expenses. *All* business expenses should go into the computation of your fees. In so far as consulting firms are concerned, overhead is broken down into two categories: (1) client-related expenses and (2) general expenses. Client-related expenses are incurred on the client's behalf and are billed directly to the client's account *in addition to* your consulting fee. General expenses are incurred on behalf of your business and are absorbed by the business *through* your fees. The main difference between the two categories is that client-related expenses are fully reimbursable, whereas general expenses must be covered by the fees you charge. For more information on business expenses and how they pertain to your record keeping and taxes, see Chapter 14.

Profit

Some consultants set their fees high enough to cover their salary and overhead requirements but neglect to consider their profits. Either they don't realize the error, or they believe that their profits are already included in their salaries. This is not the case. As an entrepreneur and risk taker, you are entitled to receive a profit on top of your salary. This is justified by the fact that you are assuming more responsibility and exposing yourself to more risk than you would if you were merely an employee. Depending on the type of consulting work you do, your profit should be between 10 and 25 percent of your combined salary and overhead. If your services are unique and there is a high demand for them, your profit may exceed this range. To determine the amount of profit you should receive for your efforts, find out what's standard for your consulting field. You can obtain this information by talking to other consultants or by contacting the professional associations for your field.

Competition

Your consulting firm doesn't exist in a vacuum. In computing your fees, you must also keep in mind what your competitors charge for similar services. This is particularly important whenever you are in a bidding situation in which the contract goes to the lowest qualified bidder. To get a better idea of the fee range for your type of consulting services, use any and all of these sources of information: other consultants, professional associations, former clients of consultants, and business leaders in your community.

Once you have ascertained the acceptable fee range for the type and quality of services you are prepared to offer, you can set your fees accordingly, opting for the low, middle, or top portion of the range. Don't assume that by setting your fees at the lowest possible level you will automatically get business. Although this may be true in bidding situations, it isn't always true in other situations. A price that's too low can be as much of a turnoff to prospective clients as a price that's too high. Low fees are often equated with low value or inferior services. We learned this the hard way. When we were just starting out as consultants, we lost a much-wanted account because our fees were too low. Fortunately, the client told us why we didn't get the job. As a result, we raised our fees.

The Economy

A pricing strategy that fails to consider the state of the economy will be doomed from the start. In addition to reflecting your costs and the competition, your fees should also reflect the economic environment in which you operate. You must consider, for instance, any increases or decreases in interest rates, changes in the tax laws, the rate of inflation, employment trends, consumer spending and savings patterns, and productivity levels. When prospective clients are experiencing strong economic periods, fees alone are rarely the deciding factor in choosing a consultant. During weak economic periods, it's another matter. Given the need to reduce costs, clients are more inclined to comparison shop, looking for consultants whose fees match their budgets. To keep your fees in line with the economy, it's essential that you be aware of the economic changes that are occurring and of their effect on your clients.

TYPES OF FEES ARRANGEMENTS

Depending on the nature of the consulting work you do or the individual requirements of particular assignments, you may opt to use one fee arrangement or another. Payments are most commonly made on (1) an hourly rate, (2) a per-project basis, (3) a retainer agreement, (4) a performance basis, or (5) an equity basis.

Hourly Rate

Consultants and clients alike often favor using an hourly rate because of its versatility and simplicity. From the consultant's point of view, arriving at a fee is just a matter of multiplying the hours spent working for the client times the rate per hour. From the client's point of view, this arrangement eliminates the need to enter into a long-term agreement with the consultant or to pay for time not received. In situations in which the client only requires services for a short period of time or sporadically, it's usually preferable to use the hourly rate.

Taking into account the factors described earlier, you can compute your hourly rate as shown here:

Salary per hour		$ ____
(your estimated worth)		
Overhead per hour	+	$ ____
(weekly total/40 hours)		
Profit per hour	+	$ ____
(____% X [salary + overhead])		
		____
Total hourly rate		$ ____

By inserting the appropriate dollar amounts on the salary, overhead, and profit lines and then adding them together, you will arrive at your total hourly rate.

Per-Project Basis

Setting your fee on a per-project basis differs from the hourly rate in that, instead of being paid for your expenditure of time, you are paid a prearranged sum for your successful completion of a specific project. In this type of arrangement, the fee that you are to receive is estimated in advance and fixed at that amount. If the project turns out to require more time than you anticipated, your fee remains unchanged. Any increase in cost must be absorbed by you. Conversely, if the project takes less time than anticipated, you still receive the full amount of the fee originally agreed on.

The per-project basis is best suited to situations in which a specific task must be carried out, such as conducting a market research survey, designing a brochure, or delivering a presentation. When you estimate the fee in advance, the client knows what to expect and doesn't have to worry about mounting costs if the project gets out of hand. This method can be advantageous to you as well. It not only rewards you for your efficiency but also simplifies your billing procedures because it does away with the need to provide the client with a breakdown of how your time was spent. To use the per-project fee arrangement effectively, you must be able to determine accurately how much of your time each project will require.

Retainer Agreement

A retainer agreement is a fee arrangement in which a client agrees to pay a consultant a predetermined monthly fee over an extended period of time (usually six months to a year). In exchange, the consultant guarantees the client a minimum number of consulting hours per month, as needed. As you can see, a retainer agreement serves basically two purposes: (1) It assures the client of having access to the consultant's services, and (2) it provides the consultant with a steady cash flow.

Retainer agreements are usually advisable in situations in which clients know they are going to need ongoing advice or assistance over a period of months. For instance, a client who needs help in developing a community-relations program, researching new markets, or analyzing investment opportunities would probably benefit from a retainer agreement. Essentially, the client eliminates any risk of your being unavailable by booking your services in advance. What's more, unlike the per-project fee arrangement, which is limited to one specific project, the retainer can cover a variety of consulting assignments over an extended period of time.

Performance Basis

In a performance basis fee arrangement, all or part of the payment you receive depends on the quality of your performance or on the result you achieve for the client.

For instance, a client hiring a consultant to institute an improved system for collecting bad debts might agree to pay the consultant a percentage of the monies collected. A training consultant brought in by a company to train newly hired employees might receive a bonus for each employee who successfully completes the training program.

For this arrangement to work, two things are necessary. First, you must have the authority to implement your recommendations or carry out the activities connected with the assignment. Second, the criteria for evaluating your performance must be measurable (i.e., monies collected, number of employees trained). To avoid disagreements later, you should agree to consult on a performance basis only when both of these stipulations have been met.

Equity Basis

In some instances, a consultant may be asked to offer his or her services in exchange for ownership in the client's business. This type of arrangement most commonly occurs when a business is still in the early stages or when it is facing bankruptcy. In both situations, the client needs the consultant's services but is not in a position to pay for them. If you agree to work on an equity basis and the business succeeds, you stand to receive far more for your efforts than you would have received from your normal fees. However, if the business fails, you could end up with nothing. Given the risk involved, equity basis fee arrangements should be entered into with extreme caution.

PAYMENT SCHEDULES

In addition to negotiating a fee arrangement with each client, you also need to establish a payment schedule specifying how and when you are to be paid for your work. For instance, a payment schedule might stipulate that you will bill the client on a monthly basis, charging for your time (at a specified hourly rate) and any client-related expenses, such as travel and long-distance phone calls. If you have agreed to work on a per-project basis and your total fee has already been determined, the payment schedule can stipulate the amount and timing of the payments you are to receive (i.e., equal payments of $4,000 due on February 1 and March 1).

Constructing a payment schedule that is mutually acceptable to you and the client isn't always easy. Ideally, the schedule you decide on should benefit both parties, helping to protect your right to be paid and the client's right to the services you promised. At the same time, the payment schedule should consider the matter of cash flow. It is important to decide reasonably who should have use of the money while the consulting assignment is being performed. Obviously, you would prefer to receive full payment in advance before starting the assignment because this gives you immediate use of the money and avoids any collection problems later. The client, on the other hand, wants to delay making payment until after the assignment is completed, thereby retaining use of the money and control over your work. To satisfy both of you, some form of compromise is needed.

Progress Payments

Most consultants find that the best way to resolve the payment issue is to ask for progress payments. Instead of receiving your total fee up front or after the assignment is over, you receive periodic payments at various stages throughout the assignment. Billing on a monthly basis, as described earlier, is a standard practice for assignments that are spread out over a number of months. Another widely used payment schedule, which we strongly recommend when possible, is to require payment in thirds. Under this arrangement, you are paid one-third of your total fee prior to starting the assignment. The second third is paid to you midway through the assignment. The final third is paid to you on completion of the assignment or within 30 days thereafter. The advantage of this method is that it links the payments you receive to your output. Although you don't have to actually *do* anything to receive the first payment, this is regarded as good-faith money in that it proves the client's ability and willingness to pay for your services. If payment in thirds isn't feasible (either because a fixed fee hasn't been determined or because another payment schedule is more suitable), it's still a good idea to request part of your fee up front. This is particularly advisable when you haven't worked with the client before or you have doubts about the client's credit.

MAXIMIZING YOUR PROFITABILITY

Even consultants who are good at setting fees and establishing payment schedules can inadvertently let profits slip through their fingers. On paper it looks as though they are achieving their full profit potential, but in reality they are not. Why? Because certain mistakes, commonly made in consulting practices, are cutting into their profits. These mistakes include the following:

1. *Not charging for advice.* Consultants often make the mistake of giving away their advice rather than selling it. This is most likely to occur when you are trying to convince a potential client to use your services. What usually happens in this instance is that the consultant, in an effort to demonstrate his or her abilities, provides too much information. Then, having in effect told the client everything already, the consultant's services are no longer needed.

2. *Providing additional services not included in the original agreement.* Once an assignment is under way, the consultant may discover that there are more facets to it than expected. As a result, more work is required. An example is the marketing consultant who is hired to create a brand name for a new product and ends up designing the package, too. If you find yourself in this situation, rather than not doing the additional work or doing it at no extra charge, you should bring your findings to the client's attention. Then, if the client wants you to perform the additional services, you can recalculate your fee to include them.

3. *Failing to bill the client for travel time.* Consultants have been known to spend four hours driving to and from a client's office and then bill the client for only a one-hour meeting. One way to get around this type of situation is to have the client come to *your* office, thereby eliminating the time you would spend commuting. Another way is to establish a minimum fee for your services that includes your travel time.

4. *Not keeping track of client-related expenses.* Consultants rarely need to be reminded to keep a record of their air travel and hotel expenses while working on an assignment, but what about long-distance phone calls, postage, typing, photocopying, materials purchased, and more? The everyday expenses you incur on the client's behalf must be accounted for in addition to your services. To have these expenses reimbursed by the client, you must keep detailed records (backed up by receipts), explaining why and when each expense was incurred. To simplify matters and ensure that their expenses are covered, some consultants add a "handling charge," which is a flat percentage of all fees due, to the client's bill.

5. *Using inefficient credit and collections procedures.* To maximize your profitability, it's advisable to run credit checks on new clients through one of the credit-reporting services, such as TRW or Dun & Bradstreet. Then, once you've established a payment schedule, stick to it. Many consultants get so caught up in their work that they neglect to bill in a timely manner. If clients do get behind on their bills, it's important to send out reminders without delay or, in extreme situations, to turn the matter over to a collection agency.

5

Promoting the Business

In addition to performing your consulting duties, you should plan to spend part of your time actively promoting your business. Providing good service alone isn't enough. It's important for you to identify prospective clients and to develop an overall strategy for communicating with them.

The services provided by successful consulting firms often aren't any better than those provided by firms that are struggling. What separates them? Why are some consulting firms generating healthy profits while others are barely getting by? Promotion makes the difference. The successful firms recognize the value of self-promotion and make it a point to keep prospective clients informed about what they have to offer. Rather than waiting for business to come to them, they go out to get it.

IDENTIFYING YOUR BEST PROSPECTS

In choosing your consulting field or fields, no doubt you gave considerable thought to the kinds of people or institutions who would be most likely to need your services. Your next step is to build a client profile of your best prospects: the prospective clients who show the most promise of actually retaining you as a consultant.

Building a Client Profile

A prospect is any individual, business, or organization that might be able to use your consulting services. A good prospect, however, is much more. As shown in Figure 5-1 depicting your client profile, a good prospect has three characteristics: (1) a need for your services, (2) the ability to afford them, and (3) the authorization to buy them. If any one of these requirements is missing, you probably won't get the assignment. If you do, you may have difficulty later in getting paid for your work.

Consultants, in particular, need to spend their time wisely. After all, time is your most valuable resource. Thus, you don't want to waste it trying to promote your business to bad prospects. The way to avoid this mistake is to ask yourself the following questions.

Does the Prospect Need My Services?

The most basic rule of business is this: Find a need and fill it. Taking this into consideration, your first priority should be to determine whether a prospect needs the types of consulting services you provide. Will using your services enable the prospective client to save or make money? Increase efficiency? Solve a problem? Look or feel better? Enjoy life more? Be more successful? The greater the prospect's need for your consulting services, the better your chance of winning the assignment. For instance, a catering consultant should focus on cultivating businesses or individuals who entertain a lot. A financial planner would want to identify people within a certain tax bracket who are likely to need advice on sheltering and increasing their income.

Figure 5-1 Client Profile

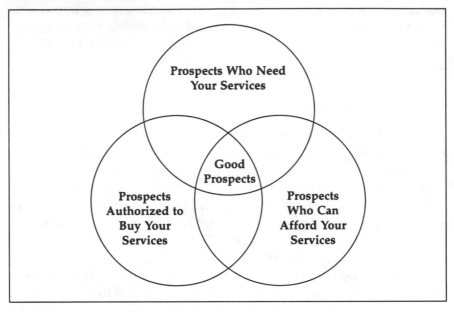

Can the Prospect Afford My Services?

Ability to pay is an important criterion in judging whether a potential client is a good prospect. This is especially true in situations in which a major portion of your fee won't be due until after your work is completed. There's no point in promoting your services to a prospect who can't afford them. Otherwise, you could succeed in getting the consulting assignment but have nothing more than a bad debt to show for it. If a prospect is unable to pay yet you still feel committed to the project, you might proceed on an equity fee arrangement. Obviously, such an arrangement entails more risk.

Is the Prospect Authorized to Buy My Services?

Just because a prospect needs and can afford your services doesn't mean that the prospect is authorized to hire you as a consultant. Someone else—a person or a committee—may be the party with the actual authority to enter into an agreement with you. All too often, consultants overlook this detail. In their eagerness to firm up an assignment, they assume that a prospect has more authority than is in fact true. For instance, a line supervisor in a factory may genuinely need the services of an air conditioning and heating specialist, and the company may be able to afford to hire such a person, but the authority to do so may actually rest with a senior-level manager. In promoting your services to businesses, you'll find that the authority to buy can be spread out over several different departments and levels of management. Depending on the scope and cost of a consulting project, it's not uncommon for as many as a dozen or more people to have a say in the buying decision. As a rule of thumb, the higher up your contacts are in an organization's management structure, the easier it will be for you to get the approvals you need.

YOUR PROMOTIONAL STRATEGY

Having identified your best prospects, your goal is to get the word out about the types of consulting services you are prepared to offer them. You will need a promotional strategy, or game plan, for communicating with the individuals depicted in your client profile. In essence, a promotional strategy is a selection process whereby you select the channels of communication that are best suited for reaching your audience. The various channels you have to choose from fall under three headings: networking, publicity, and advertising.

Networking refers to any form of personal communication you use to promote your business or yourself. It calls for you to establish and maintain a network of friends, colleagues, satisfied clients, and others who are good prospects for your consulting services or can help you reach those who are. Frequently cited by consultants as their most effective promotional tool, networking is also one of the least expensive. It is time-consuming, however. To be successful, networking requires your personal involvement and willingness to share information with the people in your network.

Publicity refers to any nonpaid form of mass communication you use to promote your business. It entails getting information about your consulting firm's services or activities reported in the news media. Such coverage is provided free of charge when the information is thought to have news value or to be of interest to the public. Publicity can be best characterized by its *three C's*: cost, control, and credibility. As indicated, there is no cost to you for the media coverage you receive. At the same time, however, you have no control over the nature of that coverage. Publicity can be favorable or unfavorable—as likely to point out your consulting firm's mistakes as its accomplishments. If a news broadcast chooses to focus on a lawsuit that's been brought against you, rather than on the prestigious award you've just won, there's little you can do about it. It's this very lack of control, though, that gives publicity its greatest strength: credibility. When the news media deliver your message, rather than a sponsor, it's much more believable.

Advertising refers to any *paid* form of mass communication you use to promote your business. In general, it involves the purchasing of print space or airtime in various communication media, such as magazines and radio. Though recognized as a necessary business communication tool, the role of advertising in promoting consulting firms is less clear. Consultants often believe that they don't need to advertise or that they shouldn't advertise. Some consider it demeaning to their professional image. Others are afraid that their clients will find it offensive. When used properly, however, advertising produces positive results. A consulting firm has as much to gain from skillful advertising as does any other business. Unlike networking or publicity, advertising is the only communication method that gives you total control over the information that is directed at your audience.

Which Method Should You Use?

Which should you use: networking, publicity, or advertising? The answer is all three. For your promotional strategy to be really effective, you should use the channels of communication within each of these categories. A consultant whose promotional strategy relies on networking alone will be unable to reach contacts outside his or her present network. Relying too heavily on publicity to communicate with prospective clients will result in a promotional strategy that's lacking in continuity and control. If you use only advertising, you will be missing out on the opportunity to meet prospective clients firsthand or to get free media exposure for your consulting practice. Networking expands your personal contacts. Publicity helps to build your reputation. Advertising provides control and a sense of direction.

NETWORKING, PUBLICITY, AND ADVERTISING

Figure 5-2 shows the networking, publicity, and advertising methods you can use to promote your consulting practice. Depending on the types of consulting you do, your audience, and the money available for promotion, some methods will be more suitable than others.

Networking

The networking methods that follow will help you make contact with prospects for your consulting services. Some of these methods can also be used to generate publicity.

Phone Calls

AT&T's former ad campaign advising people to "reach out and touch someone" has particular relevance for consultants. Using the telephone to strengthen existing relationships and to establish new ones is one of the best ways to promote your business. When you come across information that might be of value to someone in your network (or someone you would like to have in your network), call that person. Letting others know that you have their best interests in mind and are familiar with their concerns often leads to future consulting assignments.

Figure 5-2 Networking, Publicity, and Advertising Methods

Networking

Phone calls
Letters
Association memberships
Speeches and seminars
Civic and social events
Computer connections

Publicity

Media interviews
Published articles
Newsletters
Books
Awards
Charitable donations
Timely events

Advertising

Yellow pages
Direct mail
Directory listings
Newspapers
Magazines
Radio
Television
Sales promotion
   Business cards
   Brochures
   Advertising specialty items
   Trade shows

Letters

Letters perform much the same promotional function as phone calls, but they allow you to send more detailed information. We frequently send out newspaper clippings, reports, and other materials we think will be of interest to the recipients. Although this takes time, the response (and additions to our client list) has been well worth our efforts.

Association Memberships

There's no substitute for actually meeting the leaders in your particular industry or profession and having the opportunity to exchange ideas and information. Associations make this possible, bringing people together and providing forums for discussion. To take full advantage, find out which professional or trade associations best serve your needs, and then plan to join at least one. It's also a good idea to join a group where you can meet people in fields outside your own, such as the Chamber of Commerce, Rotary Club, or Women in Business.

Speeches and Seminars

Attending a speech or seminar enables you to accomplish two things at once: you gain additional information, and you make new contacts. Taking this one step farther, why not give speeches or conduct seminars yourself? This can be an extremely effective tool for promoting your consulting services and enhancing your reputation as an expert in your field. To achieve the best results, try to determine which topics hold the greatest interest for the people you want to reach. Whenever you give a speech or conduct a seminar, make it a point to get the name and addresses of those in attendance. In addition, by notifying the press of an upcoming speaking engagement or seminar, you should be able to obtain media coverage. For more information about using speeches and seminars to generate additional income, see Chapter 13.

Civic and Social Events

These gatherings provide still another avenue for developing client leads. One of the advantages of this method of networking is that it enables you to meet people who ordinarily would be inaccessible or difficult to reach. Because the environment itself is relaxed, conversation is relatively easy. Don't make the mistake of trying to deliver your sales presentation then and there when you meet someone who appears to be a good prospect. This is generally considered to be in poor taste at nonbusiness events. Instead, follow up the meeting with a phone call or letter inviting further discussion.

Computer Connections

Another way to stay in touch or increase your visibility is to go on-line and connect via computer bulletin boards, e-mail, the Internet, and other electronic means. In many consulting fields, this is the preferred way to network.

Publicity

You can use the following publicity methods to obtain media exposure for your business. In deciding which methods to use, pick those that are most compatible with your own abilities and personal preferences.

Media Interviews

The media frequently turn to outside experts for advice and information when putting together radio and television talk shows or researching newspaper and magazine articles. Making yourself available for media interviews is a way to reach thousands or even millions of people. The more relevant your information is to a program's or publication's audience, the better your chance of being interviewed. The trick is to anticipate what an audience wants to know and then adapt your information accordingly. For instance, suppose you were a banking consultant interested in being interviewed by a well-known business publication or in appearing on a daytime television talk show. In approaching the business publication, you might stress your knowledge of current banking trends and the reasons behind recent interest rate fluctuations. The talk show, on the other hand, given its high percentage of female viewers, might prefer information on the specific credit laws that protect women.

Published Articles

Writing newspaper and magazine articles on subjects within your area of expertise is another way to get public recognition. If a newspaper or magazine thinks highly enough of your views to publish them, readers are assured that you must be an expert in your field. To really capitalize on this type of publicity, you should write for the publications whose readers are good prospects for your services. Don't spread yourself too thin. Consultants who try to be experts in several fields quickly lose their credibility. An investment consultant who is known for writing articles on the securities market shouldn't write about physical fitness, unless it's "Wall Street Reacts to the Physical-Fitness Craze." To find out more about getting published and how articles can also be a source of income, read Chapter 13.

Newsletters

Another way to reach prospective clients and gain the attention of the media is to publish your own newsletter. It should consist of four to eight pages and be published on a monthly, bimonthly, or quarterly basis. The information it contains should be timely and of use to those who receive it. Your first goal is to use the newsletter to maintain contact with prospects for your consulting services. Your second is to increase your media coverage; through its distribution, you may be quoted or even interviewed. Besides publicity, newsletters can also generate additional income. For more information, see Chapter 13.

Books

Writing a book demands a much greater investment of your time than writing an article or publishing a newsletter, but the publicity value can be enormous. As a published author, you become more attractive to the media simply because the book can certify your expert status. Publishing a book also increases your chance of being quoted or interviewed. The closer the subject is to your areas of specialization, the better. Ideally, many of the same people who read the book will also contact you regarding consulting assignments. See Chapter 13 for more information on books and how they can add to your income.

Awards

Winning an award can result in publicity, too, because it lets others know that you have done something special that warranted recognition. Awards are generally given on the basis of professional achievements or volunteer service to the community. Although there's no guarantee you will win an award, you *can* shift the odds in your favor. Entering contests sponsored by professional associations in your field is one way. Becoming an active participant in a civic or charitable group is another.

Charitable Donations

Donating your consulting services to a worthy cause is one of the nicest ways to get publicity. The people who receive your services benefit, and so do you. For instance, a career guidance consultant might help high school students chart their career paths. A nutritionist could show senior citizens how to prepare simple, inexpensive, nourishing meals. These are the types of newsworthy stories that appeal to local newspapers and television news programs.

Timely Events

A promotional method often used with success by businesses is linking their publicity efforts to a timely event. Christmas, the World Series, even Tax Day can be used. The more creative your approach, the better. One investment counselor gets extensive media coverage every Christmas. Each year, he sends out a press release with his estimates of what it would cost, in current dollars, to buy all the gifts included in the song "The Twelve Days of Christmas." A special-effects make-up expert in the motion picture industry uses Halloween to its best advantage by demonstrating his talents on the five o'clock news to show how movie monsters are made.

Advertising

Each of the following advertising methods has its strengths and limitations. In choosing one medium or another, try to determine which one will enable you to reach your audience most effectively.

Yellow Pages

Any business that has a telephone is entitled to a free listing in the yellow pages section of the telephone book. In addition to this, for greater visibility, you may also want to purchase a display ad to promote your services. Some consultants, such as graphic designers, real estate appraisers, catering consultants, and insurance specialists, use this method with great success. Others, however, claim that the results don't justify the expense. For instance, management consultants, attorneys, accountants, and others who frequently get their clients through referrals, usually do not fare as well with yellow pages advertising. In our own case, we found that, although we got more telephone calls because of the yellow pages, few of the calls actually resulted in consulting assignments. More often than not, the callers wanted to sell us *their* services or had us confused with some other type of consultant in a different field.

The main advantage of yellow pages advertising is its ability to reach people within a certain geographic area at the time when they want to buy. Having already recognized a need for a particular product or service, they are just looking for the right place to buy it. Thus, given the "presold" nature of its audience, an ad in the yellow pages is essentially an attention-getting device. Your purpose is not only to provide information about the type of consulting work you do, but also to differentiate yourself from the competition. It's important to emphasize what sets you apart from other consultants in your field: experience, resources and capabilities, awards won, or whatever.

Direct Mail

This form of advertising involves printed material, such as a letter or brochure, that is mailed directly to your prospective clients. Chief among direct mail's strengths are its selectivity and flexibility. These enable you to send any promotional message to anyone at any time. In addition, direct mail provides one of the best means of explaining and describing what your consulting firm does. For example, you can use direct mail to

- Maintain client contact
- Reach new clients
- Develop your image
- Introduce new consulting services

Direct mail does have one serious limitation, however. If you aren't careful, the people who receive your materials may regard them as junk mail and throw them away. Thus, your primary concern in using direct mail should be to get your advertisement into the right hands. One point on which all marketing experts agree is that the success of any direct-mail campaign rests largely on the quality of its mailing list. The better your mailing list, the better the response to your advertisement.

You can either build your own mailing list or buy one from a list broker. If you decide to build the list yourself, you can use sources such as these: present clients, client leads you have received, business cards, organization directories, public announcements, and government records. For information on list brokers, check the "Standard Rate and Data Service," a monthly publication available at many libraries. This directory will tell you which companies specialize in preparing the type of mailing list you need.

Directory Listings

A number of publishing companies and trade and professional associations print directories that contain listings of various types of consultants. For instance, there are directories that list consultants in such fields as financial planning, advertising, interior design, management, and banking. It may be possible to have information about your consulting firm and its capabilities included in one or more directories. When a directory is published by a trade or professional association, the listings in it are usually provided free of charge to members. Nonmembers are either excluded from the directory or required to pay a fee to obtain a listing. When a publishing company compiles and distributes a directory, you may or may not have to pay a fee to be included.

If you are contemplating obtaining a directory listing, first determine what the fee, if any, will be for it. Second, find out how many copies of the directory will be printed and who will receive them. After all, there's no benefit in being listed in a directory that no one will see. Ideally, the people who subscribe to the directory should be your prospective clients.

Newspapers

Approximately 30 percent of all advertising dollars spent in the United States goes toward newspaper advertising. Part of the appeal of newspapers is that their advertising rates are generally low, and they are one of the most effective ways of reaching a local audience. In addition, newspapers tend to have an upscale readership. Researchers have found that people who read newspapers are usually better educated and earn higher incomes than those who don't.

Just placing an ad in a newspaper is no guarantee that your intended audience will read it. Readers frequently jump from one page to the next, merely glancing at ads or skipping them altogether. To catch the reader's eye, it's essential to position your ad in a way to increase its exposure and heighten its effectiveness. Known as *preferred positioning*, this technique entails placing your ad in the section of the newspaper that is most often read by your prospective clients. For instance, a catering consultant might place an ad in either the food section or the entertainment section. A computer consultant could specify the business section. Another positioning tip recommended by advertising experts is to place your ad on a right-hand page whenever possible, preferably above the fold. In this position, more people will actually notice it.

Magazines

The main advantage of magazines as a promotional vehicle is their selectivity. Given the large number of special-interest, trade, and professional magazines available, there's practically one for every audience. By choosing the magazines that most appeal to your prospective clients, you're virtually assured of getting your message across to the right people. Because people frequently save magazines for future reference after they've read them, magazine ads tend to have a long life span.

On the down side, magazines have a long *lead time*: the interval between the time your ad is placed and the date it actually appears. Magazine ads must usually be received two or three months prior to publication. Just as with newspapers, positioning is important. Without proper positioning, your ad could easily be overlooked.

To find out which magazines reach your prospective clients, check the "Standard Rate and Data Service" publications described earlier. They will provide information about each magazine's readership and advertising rates.

Radio

Radio, though not one of the more popular advertising methods among consultants, shouldn't be ignored entirely. For one thing, it is the most pervasive of the media, able to reach people wherever they are, whatever they are doing. At home, at work, driving in the car, or on vacation, people have their radios with them. In the United States today, there are almost two radios per person, and 99 percent of all households have at least one radio.

Like magazines, radio offers a high degree of selectivity, because different stations and programs appeal to different audiences. Financial planners and accountants, for example, can reach prospective clients by advertising on radio programs devoted to business and financial news. Personnel consultants, on the other hand, might purchase air time on the kind of "easy listening" stations that are frequently broadcast in office buildings.

The main drawbacks to radio advertising are the costs and complexity of the medium. To be effective, a commercial must be broadcast repeatedly over a period of weeks or months. This repetition can be expensive. As for the complexity, putting together an effective commercial usually requires professional assistance. Fortunately, many radio stations provide this assistance to advertisers at little or no charge. By advertising on smaller stations—mainly, the FM stations—you should be able to minimize your costs because their rates are lower than those of the big stations.

Television

Little need be said about the impact of television on an audience or about its ability to shape attitudes and change opinions. Currently, 98 percent of all U.S. households have one or more television sets, and the average family watches TV for almost seven hours per day.

Top-rated programs can and do reach upward of 40 million viewers week after week.

The numbers are attractive, but along with the large numbers come television's high advertising rates. Television, like radio, is known for its cost and complexity. Most consultants would be hard pressed to pay the price to advertise on network television. *Local television* and *cable television* are another matter. Many consultants are discovering that these are viable and affordable alternatives for promoting their businesses. Besides charging considerably lower rates than network television, local and cable television offer advertisers a greater degree of selectively in reaching prospective clients. To find out more about advertising on local or cable television and whether this meets your needs and budget, check the "Standard Rate and Data Service" publications.

Sales Promotion

Sales promotion is generally regarded as a supplement to advertising and includes such diverse promotional methods as business cards, brochures, advertising specialty items, and participation in trade shows.

Business Cards.   Your business card can be a strong promotional tool, defining the nature of your consulting services and enabling prospective clients to contact you. Properly wording the information on your card will increase its effectiveness. So will choosing a card design that suits your image. Some consultants use business cards that are actually miniphotographs depicting themselves in action or surrounded by the tools of their trade. A banking consultant might be shown inside a bank vault surrounded by money, an import-export specialist standing on the dock next to a shipment of merchandise. These cards cost a bit more, but if they get results, the added expense is justified.

Brochures.   In some businesses, a brochure outlining your capabilities, accomplishments, and background is essential. It helps legitimize your consulting practice and gives prospective clients something to refer to in evaluating whether to retain your services. Usually an 8.5-by-11-inch sheet of quality paper, folded in thirds and printed on both sides, should do the job. After you've determined what to include in the brochure (a description of your services, biographical information, partial client list, and so on), check with several printers to find out what each would charge to print the quantity you need or print them yourself using a desktop publishing program and the various specialty paper stocks that are available.

Advertising Specialty Items.   An advertising specialty item is any object imprinted with your consulting firm's name and phone number and given to prospective clients. The most common types of specialty items are pens, pencils, memo pads, and key chains. Ideally, the item should be inexpensive, useful, and in keeping with your image. For example, engineering consultants might give out metric conversion tables.

Trade Shows.   Purchasing exhibit space at trade shows, conventions, and conferences is another way to reach prospective clients. Consultants whose services are directed at specific industries (construction, transportation, and insurance, for instance) can use industry trade shows to communicate with decision makers in these fields. Business development conferences also frequently prove to be good sources of client leads, particularly for consultants in such areas as data processing, direct mail, and sales training.

6

Meeting with Clients

The way that you conduct yourself in meetings will have a direct bearing on your ability to win and retain clients. Meetings are an integral part of consulting. They provide consultants and clients with the opportunity to come face to face with each other, to ask questions, exchange information, and explore and develop positive working relationships. As such, the time you put into preparing for and participating in meetings should be regarded as time well spent.

To use meetings to their best advantage will require all of your skills, both as a consultant and as a communicator. In addition to demonstrating your knowledge and expertise, you must also show clients that you understand their problems and genuinely want to help solve them. Granted, turning prospects into clients isn't easy, nor is it easy to keep current clients satisfied. However, you stand a better chance of accomplishing these goals once you learn how to make meetings work for you.

You should know about the different types of meetings that can take place, how to create a professional image, and what you can do to communicate most effectively and establish a good rapport with clients.

TYPES OF MEETINGS

As a consultant, you are likely to find yourself involved in networking meetings, initial consultations, formal presentations, updating meetings, summary meetings, and follow-up meetings.

Networking Meeting

The goal of networking meetings is to maintain current business relationships or establish contact with prospective clients. Unlike the other types of meetings, they are relatively unstructured and usually take place in a relaxed atmosphere, such as a restaurant. They may occur in conjunction with an event sponsored by a trade or professional association—at a convention or conference. During a networking meeting, any overt selling or demonstrating of your consulting services should usually be minimal. Your main goal is to find out about the activities in which the person you are meeting with is presently involved and to develop client leads that you can follow up later.

Initial Consultation

The initial consultation occurs when a consultant and a prospective (or new) client have their first formal meeting. It is normally scheduled by appointment and can take place in your office or the client's. The meeting's purpose is generally of an exploratory nature, to determine the extent of the client's needs and the role that you, as the consultant, might have in fulfilling those needs. In this meeting, it is not only acceptable for you to try to sell the client on your consulting services; it is *expected*. Depending on the outcome of this meeting, you may be (1) retained as a consultant, (2) asked to prepare a formal presentation or proposal outlining the services you are qualified to provide, or (3) told that the client is unable to make a decision at this time.

Formal Presentation

The more complex a situation is, or the more people who are involved in the hiring decision, the more likely it is that you will be asked to give a formal presentation. During a formal presentation, clients want to see specifics. You will be expected, at the very least, to answer these questions: What do you intend to do? How long will it take you to complete the assignment? What will you accomplish? How much will your services cost?

Visual aids, samples of your work, statistics, case histories of similar assignments you have performed, and other such evidence of your expertise can come into play in a formal presentation. For example, it's standard for advertising consultants to bring samples of the ads they have helped to create. Risk management consultants, on the other hand, would probably rely on statistics to show how they can reduce the number of accidents and lower insurance premiums. In addition to the presentation itself, you may also be called on to submit a detailed, written proposal explaining your approach to the situation. For more information on proposals, see Chapter 7.

Updating Meeting

The purpose of updating meetings is to keep the client informed of your progress once you have started work on an assignment. During an updating meeting, you can describe what you have already accomplished and explain what you plan to do next. This is also the time to ask or answer any questions that arise. Depending on the terms of your agreement and the duration of the assignment, the number of updating meetings that take place can vary. In some instances, you may not need to schedule any meetings. In others, especially when the assignment is a lengthy one, you might schedule several meetings spread out over a period of months.

Summary Meeting

At the conclusion of an assignment, it's often helpful to have a summary meeting with the client. This provides an opportunity for you to submit any remaining work or information that is due and for the client to ask questions. Based on the complexity of the assignment and what still needs to be discussed, a summary meeting can last anywhere from an hour to several days. The format of the meeting itself can range from a casual discussion over lunch to an elaborate presentation with audiovisuals. Although a summary meeting signifies the end of an assignment, successful consultants are often able to use the meeting as a springboard to future assignments. To do this, you must listen carefully to what the client is saying and try to read between the lines to detect any additional needs the client may have.

Follow-up Meeting

Follow-up meetings generally take place two to four weeks after an assignment has been completed. The goal is to let the client know that you stand behind the consulting services you provide. Rather than walking away from a completed assignment, you are interested in obtaining the client's feedback and are willing to offer additional assistance if it is needed. It's true that follow-up meetings require more of your time without any guarantee of increased revenues, but they go a long way toward satisfying clients, and in so doing they help to generate repeat business and client referrals.

Each type of meeting just described involves the exchange of a specific kind of information and serves its own unique purpose. Some consulting assignments include all six types of meetings. Other assignments call for only some of the meetings. In theory, each type of meeting should dovetail into the next. Of course, it won't always happen this way. Not all networking meetings result in actual consulting assignments, and not all assignments require formal presentations or updating meetings. Instead of arranging a follow-up meeting to obtain the client's feedback, you may prefer to make a phone call or write a letter. Whatever the situation, the greater your awareness of how and when to use the various types of meetings, the better equipped you will be to profit from them.

CREATING A PROFESSIONAL IMAGE

Given the personal nature of consulting work—you are the business—it's extremely important to define and cultivate your professional image. Not only must the image you decide on match the expectations of your clients, but it must be compatible with your personality as well. The type of professional image that's suitable for a graphic designer differs from the image that's suitable for a tax consultant. The graphic designer needs to project an image that tells clients, "I possess the originality, creativity, and artistic skills necessary to get the job done. You are going to love my work." The tax consultant, on the other hand, needs a professional image that says, "Don't worry. I know the tax laws inside and out, and I can save you money. Trust me." The professional image you project to others is actually a combination of four separate components: words, actions, appearance, and environment.

Words

The words you use to address clients and to describe your consulting services, along with your tone of voice, add to your professional image. Through your choice of words, you can increase your credibility as an expert in your field and can help put clients at ease. To achieve these ends, always make it a point to speak to clients with courtesy and respect. In discussing your work, explain the relevant details clearly and concisely, providing clients with an opportunity to ask questions. Rather than trying to razzle-dazzle clients with recitations of your abilities, give your accomplishments a chance to speak for themselves.

Actions

Your actions can serve as a bridge to bring you and the client closer together or as a barrier to keep you apart. In your effort to present yourself as a professional, don't make the mistake of acting aloof or condescending. Successful consultants feel confident enough to treat clients as equals. At the same time, they always take the client's needs into consideration. For example, if a meeting is set to take place in your office, have all the materials you will need at hand so you won't have to waste the client's time looking for them. Then, before you begin to talk business, make sure that the client is comfortable. Offering coffee or tea is a nice gesture. Providing pens and paper for the client to take notes is another. By these actions and others, you not only show your concern for the client, but demonstrate your competence and sense of control.

Appearance

Appearance is another facet of your professional image. Your attire and grooming tell clients a great deal about you, making a statement about your personality and even the quality of your consulting services. Despite warnings that it's wrong to judge a book by its cover, this is precisely what people do. First impressions *are* important. The more closely your appearance conforms to clients' expectations of how a successful consultant should look, the easier it will be for you to gain their confidence.

This isn't to say that there is only one look that is acceptable for consultants or that you shouldn't be allowed to express your personal taste and preferences in fashion. To achieve the right effect, you should adopt a style that is acceptable to you and the client. In comparing the appearance of the graphic designer and the tax consultant, mentioned earlier, two very different looks are likely to emerge. The graphic designer's clothing and accessories should convey a feeling of innovativeness and flair, whereas the tax consultant's attire should be more traditional, suggesting fiscal responsibility and good business sense.

Environment

Your work environment itself is also part of your professional image. Something as simple and basic as a desk can send a message to clients about the type of person you are and how you will approach a consulting assignment. For example, two desks of equal value—one constructed out of chrome and glass, the other made of dark mahogany—can present very different images. The first conveys a futuristic feeling and says that the owner is unconventional and an original thinker: the perfect image for the graphic designer. The second evokes a feeling of permanence and says that the owner is responsible and practical: not a bad image for the tax consultant. Depending on the other furnishings that surround each desk, these images an be reinforced or modified. Thus, the starkness of the chrome and glass can be softened by the addition of a comfortable sofa nearby. Any stodginess associated with the mahogany desk might be downplayed by hanging a modern painting on the wall. Whatever your environment, whether it's functional or formal, high-tech or traditional, you want it to help facilitate your relationship with clients. Rather than drawing attention to itself, it should serve as a backdrop for you, enhancing your professional image and adding to your credibility as a consultant.

COMMUNICATING EFFECTIVELY

The basis for establishing a rewarding consultant-client relationship ultimately comes down to one thing: communication. To work together, you and the client must be able to communicate with each other. The suggestions that follow should help you to communicate more effectively with clients and strengthen your ability to promote and provide your consulting services.

1. *Put yourself in the client's position.* Good communicators know the importance of empathy: being able to see a situation from the other person's point of view. Granted, the client has come to you for your ideas and perspective, but without first gaining an understanding of how the client perceives the situation, you can't begin to establish a dialogue. To communicate more effectively, you should approach new client relationships with an open mind, putting preconceptions behind and allowing each client to tell his or her story.

2. *Don't overlook the nonverbal messages you are sending.* Your words may be saying one thing, but your body language (facial expressions, posture, gestures) may be saying something else. For example, avoiding the client's eyes after you've quoted your fee sends a message—that the fee is too high or that you haven't told the client everything. Tapping your fingers on a desk surface tells clients you are impatient. Shuffling papers usually indicates nervousness.

3. *Remember that the communication process is two-sided.* In addition to being a good speaker, you must also be a good listener. Once the client has received your input, it's up to you to interpret the feedback that is generated. Is the client's response to what you have just said positive or negative? Undecided? Is additional information needed? What doubts or uncertainties still exist? The better you are at interpreting and responding to the client's feedback, whether it's verbal or nonverbal, the better you will be at convincing the client of your views.

4. *Ask questions.* As a consultant, you expect the client to ask you questions, but what about the opposite? Answering questions is only half of your role. To obtain a thorough understanding of the client's situation, you must also be able to *ask* questions. This "probing" entails getting clients to open up and reveal the types of information you need to carry out your assignment. You will find that probing not only helps you get at the facts of the matter, but also helps you develop a rapport with the client by emphasizing the collegial aspects of your relationship.

5. *Think before you speak.* During meetings or phone conversations with clients, avoid the urge to "shoot from the lip." It's better to tell a client that you need additional time to check your facts or gather the necessary information than to give an inaccurate or incomplete answer. The same applies to making suggestions or identifying problems. Resist the temptation to give on-the-spot, instant analyses of situations before you have had a chance to formulate your thoughts and weigh the various alternatives. The ability to think and act quickly is an asset, but so is having the patience to do an assignment correctly.

6. *Be enthusiastic.* If you aren't enthusiastic about your consulting services, why should the client be? In communicating with the client, it's important for you to get the point across that you enjoy your work and are eager to use your abilities on the client's behalf. This doesn't mean resorting to phoniness or hype, but simply showing the client that you will tackle the assignment with the energy and enthusiasm it deserves.

7. *Personalize the relationship.* Address clients by their names, rather than constantly referring to them as *you.* When personal information is revealed, such as a client's hobbies, plans for an upcoming trip, or details about family members, make a mental note of it so you can refer to it at a later date. This lets clients know that you value them as individuals and not just "accounts."

8. *Be prepared.* This motto has as much relevance for consultants as it does for scouts. To communicate effectively, you must have something to say. Do your research in advance, and have access to the materials and information you will need to get your points across and answer the client's questions. Few things can be more damaging to the consultant-client relationship than showing up for meetings unprepared or failing to anticipate the client's concerns. The key word here is *anticipate.* In addition to reacting to the client's current needs, try to foresee any new ones on the horizon, and be prepared to satisfy them.

9. *Provide tangible proof of what you can do.* In addition to the usual facts and figures, it helps to appeal to the client's five senses: the ability to hear, see, touch, smell, and taste. Food-related services are a natural for this technique. For example, catering consultants

shouldn't just describe the various dishes they prepare but should show color photographs of them attractively displayed—or, better yet, offer clients samples to taste. With a little imagination, other types of consulting services can also be made to appeal to the senses. Sales-training consultants can demonstrate their abilities by showing prospective clients videocassettes of their training sessions. Computer consultants can use the hands-on approach by getting clients to sit at the computer and actually operate it.

10. *Emphasize benefits, rather than features.* Features describe your consulting services; benefits are the advantage the client will derive from using them. The essential difference, as shown in the following examples, is that benefits give the client a reason to buy.

Features	*Benefits*
Our firm specializes in office design and layout.	Changing your layout will increase employee morale and productivity.
I advise clients on the computers and software that are available.	I will select and install the best computer system for your needs.
This physical-fitness program includes instruction in both diet and exercise.	After completing the program, you'll see a noticeable improvement in your stamina and appearance.
I provide companies with government procurement information.	I will show you how you can win government contracts.
My public relations firm represents several major corporations.	I can get your company the media exposure it deserves.
I'll examine all aspects of your credit and collection procedures.	In similar situations, I've improved clients' collection rates by up to 30 percent.
As a catering consultant, I know what goes into planning a dinner party.	Your dinner party will be a huge success.
We'll set up and monitor your inventory control system.	Inventory shortages and surpluses will be a thing of the past.

As you can see, instead of focusing on what your services are, you want to communicate what your services can do for the client.

7

Preparing Proposals, Contracts, and Reports

Proposals, contracts, and reports are the tools of the consultant's trade. They enable you to package and present your services, define the terms of your agreements, and apprise clients of your progress. By developing the ability to express yourself through these written materials, you can work more harmoniously with clients and enhance your standing as a consultant.

PROPOSALS THAT SELL

Before entering into an agreement, more often than not, clients will want you to prepare a proposal explaining the consulting services you wish to provide. The purpose of such a proposal is twofold: (1) It provides the client with the necessary information to reach a decision, and (2) it serves as a vehicle for promoting your services. To achieve the best results, your proposals should

- Define the client's situation as you see it, emphasizing the problems that need to be solved or the actions that need to be taken
- Outline the steps you would take to remedy the situation
- Establish yourself as the person most qualified to carry out the assignment
- Highlight the benefits to be derived from using your services

Based on your understanding of the client's needs and budget, your proposal may be quite detailed, going so far as to specify how and when the work would be completed and what your fees and payment schedule would be. In this instance, your proposal closely resembles a letter of agreement, and in fact, if both parties sign it, the proposal can become a binding contract. When you have only a general idea of what the client wants, your proposal should be less specific, describing your consulting services in broader terms. Later, once you and the client have clarified the situation, you can expand your original proposal or incorporate the additional information into a written contract.

What to Put in Your Proposal

Part of the secret to writing proposals is to make them as "reader friendly" as possible. You should anticipate the reader's questions and concerns and should supply the appropriate specifics to answer them. Your proposal should also be well organized and professional in appearance. As for the length of a proposal, this can vary in accordance with the size and dollar value of the project. The more involved the project is, the more the reader usually expects to see. Proposals for major government projects are sometimes hundreds of pages long. However, this is the exception, rather than the rule. The majority of proposals for consulting projects range from a few pages in length to a maximum of 25 pages.

To make your proposals more acceptable to prospective clients, it helps to include certain key elements in your proposal format.

Depending on the nature of the consulting project, your proposal should contain some or all of the following elements:

Letter of Transmittal.   A letter of transmittal, or cover letter, should always accompany your proposal, even if one isn't specifically requested as part of the proposal package. This letter serves to introduce you to the prospective client and to identify your proposal.

Title Page.   This states the topic of your proposal and provides such information as your name and/or the company's name, your address and phone number, and the date the proposal was prepared. If the proposal is in response to a government Request for Proposals (RFP), additional information may be needed to identify the RFP to which your proposal pertains.

Table of Contents.   The value of a table of contents is that it tells the reader at a glance what information is included in your proposal and where to find it. Rather than having to hunt for the desired information, it is readily accessible. With short proposals of three pages or less, the table of contents is unnecessary. With longer proposals, it is essential.

Summary of the Proposal.   This section, consisting of one to two paragraphs, describes what you intend to do. It should be brief and to the point, defining the consulting project and its overall purpose.

What the Proposal Will Accomplish.   Taking your summary one step farther, this section focuses on the benefits the client will receive once your proposal has been carried out. Such benefits may include increased efficiency, cost savings, improved employee morale, or the achievement of an objective. Stating the benefits in this way makes your proposal more salable, but be careful not to promise more than you can deliver.

Scope of the Work.   This section is the real nuts and bolts of your proposal. It sets forth the proposed processes and specific tasks needed to meet the objectives of the consulting project. Your approach to the assignment and the methodology you would employ should be carefully explained. Note that you don't need to give away any trade secrets or proprietary information here but that the information you provide must be specific enough to tell the client what your work will entail.

Estimated Time Required.   Based on your knowledge of the consulting project, estimate how long it will take to complete the various tasks involved. The more you know about the project itself and the client's needs, the more specific you can be. As a rule of thumb, give yourself some leeway—a margin of 10 percent or so—in calculating the project's time span. That way, if everything doesn't go according to plan, you still have time to take corrective action.

Estimated Cost.   As was the case with your time estimate, the more you know about the project, the more closely you can estimate its cost. If your proposal is primarily an exploratory one and many of the details have yet to be resolved, you should not attempt to estimate costs at this time. To do so would not only result in an estimate of questionable accuracy, but might alienate the client. On the other hand, if the client is requesting bids or if the issue of costs has already been clarified, then try to be as specific as you can. At the same time, explain how client-related expenses are to be handled and what your billing procedures are.

Qualifications and Experience.   In this section, you should outline the qualifications and experience that make you suited to perform the proposed assignment. Citing specific education or training, similar projects successfully completed, or experience gained while working for a former employer will help to bolster your position. Background information should also be provided for any associates or subcontractors you intend to use in the project.

Adhering to this format should help increase your success rate in obtaining approvals for your proposals. To strengthen your chances even more, try following these suggestions:

1. If the proposal must be submitted by a certain deadline, make sure it reaches the client prior to that time.
2. Indicate in your letter of transmittal that the proposal is based on your current knowledge of the client's needs. State that if those needs are different or have changed, you are willing and able to modify the proposal accordingly.
3. If you haven't received an answer after a reasonable period of time (usually one to three weeks), don't be afraid to contact the client to verify the status of your proposal. You might also offer to answer any questions that the client may have concerning the proposal.
4. Don't push too hard, trying to force the client to give you an early answer. This pressure may result in an answer, but probably not the one you want.

THE CONSULTING CONTRACT

The issue of whether to use a contract can be a touchy one. On the plus side, a contract spells out the terms of your agreement with the client, helps to avert misunderstandings, and, if necessary, can be used as evidence in a court of law. On the minus side, clients are often put off by contracts, particularly lengthy ones packed with legal phrases. Instead of facilitating your agreement, these contracts distance you from the client. What's more, because the services of an attorney are usually needed to draw up a contract correctly, additional time and expense are required.

What should you do then: use a contract or not use a contract? The majority of consultants we spoke to use a variation of the formal contract, or what's known as a *letter of agreement*. We have found that this almost always meets our purposes, too. Unlike the document an attorney prepares, a letter of agreement is written in plain language on your stationery and usually isn't more than three pages long. Essentially, it's nothing more than a detailed proposal with spaces where you and the client sign, thereby accepting its terms of the agreement.

What to Put in Your Letters of Agreement

Your letters of agreement should provide at least the following information:

Names of the Parties Involved.   To be valid, the agreement must specify who is to be bound by its terms.

Consulting Services to Be Performed.   The information provided in the "summary" and "scope of the work" sections of your proposal goes here, along with any other details that are relevant to the assignment. Be as specific as you can, and whenever possible, quantify the tasks you will perform. For example, writing "Consultant will conduct focus group interviews for the client" is too vague. Who will the consultant interview? How many sessions will there be? "Consultant will interview 30 women between the ages of 18 and 45 in two three-hour focus group sessions" provides the missing details.

Start and Stop Dates.   When will you start work on the assignment, and how long will it take you to complete it? Without this information, your agreement is worthless because there must be some stipulation as to the time frame when the services will be provided. Stating that "interviews are to be conducted during the month of March" solves the problem.

Fees and Payment Schedule.   A contract is only binding when both parties give something of value to each other. Thus, you must indicate what you are to receive in exchange for your services, clarifying the fee arrangement you and the client have agreed on and the payment schedule that is to be used—for example, "Consultant is to receive $8,000, 50 percent due prior to starting the assignment and 50 percent due within 30 days after the assignment is completed."

Expenses.   Are client-related expenses to be billed to the client, or are they included in your overall fee? This obviously has a bearing on the amount of your fee and the type of fee arrangement you use.

Never assume that you will be reimbursed for expenses you incur on the client's behalf. This should be discussed ahead of time and written into your letter of agreement.

Support Services the Client Is to Provide.   The support services, if any, that the client will provide should also be listed in your agreement. They include such things as office space, secretarial assistance, telephone service, and photocopying.

In most instances, this information should be sufficient to protect your rights and the client's. However, for additional protection, you may want to clarify some additional points.

Your Employment Status.   For tax and insurance purposes, it's advisable to indicate that you are an independent contractor and not an employee. As such, you have neither the rights nor the obligations of an employee.

The Use of Subcontractors.   Make it clear whether you have the right to subcontract part of the work on the assignment to outside people or firms. In the event that this is permitted, the client may wish to retain the right of final approval over anyone you hire.

Confidentiality.   Many consulting contracts contain a clause stating that any information the client reveals to the consultant will be kept confidential. This assures clients that their privacy will be maintained and that others won't have access to their information.

Attorney's Fees.   This stipulates who will be responsible for the payment of attorney's fees should it be necessary to use an attorney to resolve any legal disputes that may arise. It's usually stated that all court and attorney's fees shall be paid by the party who does not prevail in the lawsuit.

Your letters of agreement can address other issues besides the ones described. In fact, there are probably as many different types of letters of agreement as there are different types of consultants. If you are uncertain what to include in your agreements or the correct wording to use, contact an attorney. For more information specifically related to government contracts, See Chapter 11.

REPORTS AND RECOMMENDATIONS

Reports provide a means of communicating with clients and documenting your consulting activities. During a consulting project, progress reports enable the client to follow your progress and stay actively involved in what you are working to accomplish. Once a project has been completed, a well-written *summary report* can assist the client in implementing your recommendations.

Report Guidelines

The following guidelines will help you get the most mileage out of the reports you prepare for clients.

Progress reports should

- Be timely. The main purpose of progress reports is to inform the client of the developments that are occurring throughout the consulting assignment. To achieve this end, your progress reports should coincide with the various stages of the assignment.
- Be succinct and to the point. Verbose, rambling reports not only take longer to prepare, but are generally disdained by clients. If you really want to win over clients, show your respect for their time by sticking to the facts.
- Highlight your findings or accomplishments. The discoveries you have made, the tasks you have completed—these are the meat of your progress reports. As such, they should be chronicled in an accurate and thorough manner, thus enabling the client to derive the full value from your efforts.
- Detail any problems you encountered. The client has a right to be informed of any problems you encounter in performing your consulting services because these may affect the

client. In reporting problems, try to be as objective as possible, neither minimizing the importance of a problem nor
blowing it out of proportion.

- Estimate the percentage of the work you have completed.
  Estimating the work you have completed helps to reassure
  the client that progress is being made. This estimate is particularly important on long-term projects, which, from the
  client's point of view, often seem to stretch out into infinity.
- Explain what you intend to do next. Rather than leaving the
  client in the dark, outline the steps you plan to take in the
  next phase of the assignment. Providing prior notice in this
  way increases the client's involvement in the project and
  enables you to affirm that your proposed actions are in keeping with the client's wishes.
- Offer your recommendations to date. Depending on the consulting assignment, it may be in the client's best interests to
  submit your recommendations at periodic intervals throughout the assignment instead of waiting until after your work
  is completed. If so, these recommendations should be included in your progress reports.

Summary reports should

- Provide an overview of the assignment. This sets forth the
  circumstances surrounding the consulting assignment and
  states its objectives.
- Document the activities that took place. What did you do,
  and why? Your summary report should detail the tasks that
  you performed on the client's behalf and the purposes they
  served.
- Highlight your findings and/or accomplishments. To present
  the whole picture, include both your current findings and
  those contained in any progress reports you have already
  submitted to the client. Try to be as specific as possible in
  this section, backing up your statements with the appropriate facts and figures.
- Present your recommendations. Having completed the consulting assignment, what are your recommendations? This

is the most important part of your summary report because it shows the client what needs to be done to achieve the desired objectives.

- Suggest methods of implementation. Recommendations alone may not be enough for the client. Often, what's needed is a step-by-step blueprint for carrying out the recommendations. This explains how and when the various actions should be taken.
- Emphasize the benefits the client is drawing from your efforts. To encourage the client to follow through on your recommendations, be sure to point out the benefits associated with following-through. Any benefits that the client has already received as a result of your actions should also be itemized.

8

Managing Your Time

One thing all consultants have in common, regardless of specialization, is the need to use their time effectively. Consulting is a labor-intensive business in which the primary product is time—your time. What you are able to accomplish as a consultant will largely depend on your ability to preserve this time and channel it into profitable activities. Thus, along with the other skills you possess, you must also include this one: time management.

To become more proficient at time management, start by asking yourself the all-important question, "How do I currently spend my time?" Even though consultants bill for their time and are more adept than most at accounting for it, time still has a way of getting out of hand. Projects that are estimated to require 40 hours to complete turn out to require 60 hours or more. Part of the reason for this discrepancy is that consulting generally requires you to juggle several activities at once. Rather than sticking with a single assignment until it's finished, you're likely to be working on other projects at the same time. Then there's the consulting practice itself to run. Given this intermingling of activities, it's easy to lose track of the time.

KEEPING A TIME LOG

The simplest way to find out where your time goes is to keep a daily record, or time log, detailing how each working hour is spent (Figure 8-1). By filling in a time log similar to the one shown, you can accurately determine the amount of time that you spend on each separate activity.

For instance, you may be surprised to learn that a "five-minute" phone consultation with a client actually lasted 20 minutes. The "minute or so" that it takes to go over the bills each week is closer to two hours. Time frequently does not go where it's supposed to go or where you think it has gone. Everyday interruptions, unforeseen occurrences, and emergencies have a way of eating into your time. Add to this the not-uncommon tendency of consultants to set unrealistic daily goals for themselves, fully expecting to accomplish two days' work in one day's time. Such ambition and diligence is commendable but misguided. Instead of leading to higher productivity, it leads to workaholic behavior, frustration, and eventual burnout.

After a week or two of keeping a daily time log, you should ask yourself the following questions:

- How many hours did I spend on the following:
  Consulting projects?
  Promoting my services?
  Running my office?
  Other activities?
- How many hours did I spend on activities that I would categorize as time wasters?
- What situations happened over which I had no control?
- Which activities should receive more of my time?
- Which activities should receive less of my time?
- Did I accomplish the things I set out to do?

To further keep track of your time and ensure that clients are billed properly, it's essential to maintain individual client time sheets, like the one in Figure 8-2, showing the hours you spend working for each client.

Figure 8-1 Daily Time Log

Daily Time Log   *Date* _____
                        Consulting Activities

7:00 _____   3:00 _____
     _____   _____
     _____   _____

8:00 _____   4:00 _____
     _____   _____
     _____   _____

9:00 _____   5:00 _____
     _____   _____
     _____   _____

10:00 _____   6:00 _____
     _____   _____
     _____   _____

11:00 _____   7:00 _____
     _____   _____
     _____   _____

12:00 _____   8:00 _____
     _____   _____
     _____   _____

1:00 _____   9:00 _____
     _____   _____
     _____   _____

2:00 _____   10:00 _____
     _____   _____
     _____   _____

Figure 8-2 Client Time Sheet

	FERRIS AND ASSOCIATES			
	MARKETING RESEARCH			
	CLIENT TIME SHEET			
Client's Name _____		Consulting Project _____		
Address _____				
DATE	ACTIVITY	LOCATION	CONSULTANT	HOURS

INCREASING YOUR QUALITY TIME

Knowing where your time goes is just the beginning. Increasing the amount of quality time you have to spend comes next. Quality time—when you are actively pursuing your goals creatively and constructively—can be hard to come by. To maximize the amount of quality time you have available for consulting activities, you must overcome certain obstacles. Specifically, you must reduce or eliminate as many time wasters as possible—those that you have already identified and those that you may have overlooked.

Taken individually—a minute here and a minute there—time wasters don't seem to amount to much. When totaled, however, they can actually eclipse the amount of time you spend productively. Examples of time wasters include waiting for a client who's late for an appointment, having your telephone call placed on hold, looking for a misplaced file, and resubmitting a bill that was sent to the wrong person. Each one cuts into your quality time. As shown in the following list, time wasters can be internally generated by you or externally generated by other people or outside events. An inadequate filing system, which causes you to spend too much time looking for things, is an internal time waster because you have control over it. Waiting for a client to show up for an appointment is an external time waster because you have no control over it.

Time Wasters

Internal

Unorganized desk	Lack of prioritization
Inadequate filing system	Duplicated efforts
Improper tools or equipment	Spreading yourself too thin
Inefficient work area layout	Unwillingness to delegate tasks
Poor scheduling	Unclear objectives
Failure to communicate	Inability to say no
Insufficient planning	Procrastination
Indecision	

External

Telephone interruptions	Excessive paperwork
Waiting for clients	Red tape
Equipment breakdowns	Imcompetent people
Needless meetings	Misunderstandings
Lack of information	Unclear policies and procedures
Misinformation	Holdups in obtaining approvals

Internally generated time wasters are the easiest to eliminate because they are the result of your own actions. Once these actions are changed, the time wasters disappear. Externally generated time wasters are more of a problem. Because they are beyond your control, you can't totally eliminate them. They can be minimized, but sometimes you simply need to learn how to accept them.

THE CONSULTANT'S TIME-MANAGEMENT SYSTEM

By employing the following strategies, you should be in a better position to overcome time wasters and increase your quality time.

Organize Your Work Environment

Papers, files, supplies, and equipment should all be kept in their own special places where they are out of the way but readily accessible when you need them. Equipment should be maintained at regular intervals. This way, you won't have to waste time looking for misplaced items or waiting for crucial repairs to be made.

Set Priorities

Determine in advance what goals you wish to accomplish, on both a short-term and a long-term basis, and rank them in order of importance. Then focus on the activities that must be carried out to reach the goals that have the highest priorities. Postpone work on low-priority goals until higher-ranking goals have been met.

Identify High-Productivity Hours

In allocating your time, it helps to identify the hours during the day when you are at peak efficiency. Some people work better in the morning; others don't reach their stride until the afternoon. You may find that you have periods of peak efficiency scattered throughout the day. Whatever your pattern, identify these times and reserve them, whenever possible, for the high-priority items on your list. Schedule important meetings or phone calls, planning, and creating for your most productive times of the day.

Communicate Clearly

Misunderstandings and mistakes can be costly and time-consuming. They can frequently be avoided by taking the time to communicate clearly. Just because something seems obvious to you doesn't mean it is obvious to others. Make sure that your clients understand what you are doing each step of the way. Explain what your consulting services entail as simply and concisely as you can, keeping jargon to a minimum. Ask clients to do the same with you. If you are uncertain about what a client wants done, ask him or her to explain.

Plan Meetings and Phone Calls

Meetings and phone calls are essential to doing business. Yet, as most consultants will tell you, they can also be among the biggest time wasters if they are not planned in advance. When making a phone call to a current or prospective client, decide what you want to say before placing the call. Write notes, if necessary, to remind yourself of the points you want to make. Before scheduling a meeting, ask yourself exactly what the meeting is to accomplish: provide a progress report, generate new business, or fulfill some other purpose? Then be prepared to discuss the topics that relate to the purpose at hand.

Set Time Limits

If meetings with clients are taking longer than you feel is necessary or if clients keep you waiting while they attend to something else, set time limits. Let people know that the meeting must be concluded at a certain time. Psychiatrists and psychologists frequently use the "50-minute hour," concluding therapy sessions ten minutes before the hour is up so they have time to prepare for the next meeting. This tactic may work for you. A less abrupt way of speeding things along is to tell clients that you have another appointment to keep. Billing at an hourly rate is another possibility, giving clients the option of taking up less of your time or paying you for more of it.

Learn Others' Policies and Procedures

When your clients are businesspeople, ask them to spell out their companies' policies and procedures in advance. This will reduce misunderstandings and enable you to cut through red tape more quickly. Rather than fighting the system and creating ill will in the process, you can work within the system. Note that if you are selling your consulting services to the government, playing by the rules is critical.

Use Remnant Time

Remnant time—the intervals between scheduled activities—is quite often wasted. It can be the 15-minute gap between lunch and a meeting or the half-hour wait to receive necessary information. Bit by bit, the remnant time adds up. One way to have more quality time for high-priority activities is to use these odd remnants of time to take care of low-priority or routine activities. Returning a phone call, writing a personal note, catching up on your reading, and checking supplies can be accomplished during remnant time.

Learn to Say No

By learning to say no, you can cut back not only on time wasters, but also on the stress caused by taking on too many responsibilities. The next time you are asked to join an organization or serve on a committee, stop and ask yourself these questions: Is this something I really want to do? Would it be a good use of my time? Could someone else just as easily do it? Instead of spreading yourself too thin by trying to be involved in everything, choose the activities that are most in keeping with your goals. The same applies to consulting assignments. Difficult as it is to turn business away, if you don't think an assignment is right for you, then say no to it. Otherwise, you'll end up doing the work but deriving little satisfaction from it.

Act Now

Probably the biggest time waster of all is procrastination: putting off till tomorrow what can be done today. Once you've made a decision to do something or accepted an assignment, begin to lay the groundwork for carrying it out. By acting now, rather than later, you have a better chance of actually accomplishing what you set out to do. The quality of your work should be better, too, because you won't have to rush to complete it.

SETTING PRIORITIES

In setting priorities for the things you wish to accomplish, it helps to use a daily planner containing pages similar to the one shown in

Figure 8-3. Daily planners such as the ones produced by Day Runner, Inc. and the Franklin Quest Company, enable you to rank your activities in order of importance and track the progress of each task through to completion. Activities that are not completed by the end of the day are carried over to the next day, the day after that, and so on, until eventually they are either completed or eliminated.

The important thing to remember in organizing your time is that you should always give your attention to top-priority items first. Low-priority items can be tempting, especially when they are easier to do and take up less time, but it's a mistake to start with them. If you do, you may never finish the top- and high-priority tasks. Instead of completing three low-priority items, you would do better to complete 20 percent of the work on one top-priority item.

Granted, setting priorities and sticking to them isn't easy. There will always be days when everything cries out for your immediate attention and all of your projects should have been completed yesterday. However, as your time management skills improve, these days will become fewer and farther between.

MEETING DEADLINES

Anyone who becomes a consultant must be prepared to meet deadlines. Much as you might want to ignore them, deadlines are an inescapable part of consulting life. Along with meetings, proposals, projects, and fees, they come with the territory. It's essential that your time-management system include provisions for meeting deadlines.

To keep deadlines from getting the best of you, try following these suggestions:

1. *Give yourself enough time.* When discussing deadlines, don't accept one that is unrealistically short. To do so is to set yourself up for failure.

2. *Don't have two deadlines on the same day.* It's hard enough meeting one deadline, let alone two. If doubling up is unavoidable, move one of the dates up and plan to complete one project ahead of time and the other one on time.

Figure 8-3 Daily Planner

Daily Planner___ Date _____	Schedule
Things to Do	
	7:00
_____ _____	8:00
_____ _____	9:00
_____ _____	10:00
_____ _____	11:00
_____ _____	12:00
_____ _____	1:00

	Priorities	Comments/Status	Schedule
			2:00
Top			3:00
			4:00
High			5:00
			6:00
Med.			7:00
			8:00
			9:00
Low			10:00

3. *Establish minideadlines.* Instead of trying to meet one major deadline, establish separate "minideadlines" for completing parts of the assignment. This enables you to monitor your progress and take corrective action if you start to fall behind schedule.

4. *Remember Murphy's Law.* According to Murphy, "What can go wrong, will go wrong." So when planning your schedule, leave yourself a little extra time in case something goes wrong and you're unable to work as quickly as anticipated.

5. *Ask for an extension if necessary.* Your best efforts notwithstanding, if it becomes apparent that you are going to miss a deadline, ask for an extension. Do this before you've missed the deadline, and explain the reasons for the delay (the project has grown, you're waiting for additional information, and so on). As long as your explanation is plausible, there's a good chance the client will agree to the extension.

Using a Gantt Chart

Many consultants find that the best way to keep track of an assignment's progress is with a Gantt chart. As shown in Figure 8-4, a Gantt chart is a pictorial representation of the work flow on a specific project. The chart enables you to see the separate activities that need to be done and the time frame for their completion. Not only does the chart show when each task should begin and end, but it also shows the various interrelationships among the tasks and the points at which they overlap.

Invented by Henry Gantt in the early 1900s, The Gantt chart was initially used to schedule jobs in factories. Since its invention, the chart's application has broadened considerably. It is now used by managers and consultants in virtually all fields. In addition to using the Gantt chart to outline the stages of a single project, you can also use it to compare the status of separate projects and activities. This will enable you to schedule work on one project so that it coincides with the lulls in another project. Although Gantt charts were originally prepared and updated by hand, now it can all be done by computer with one of the project-management programs that are on the market.

Figure 8-4 Gantt Chart for a Marketing Research Project

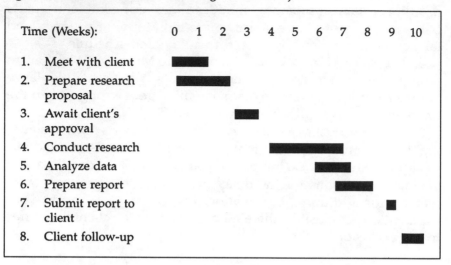

Note: The time line can be in days, weeks, or months, and the number sequence can be multiples, such as 0, 2, 4, 6, or 0, 4, 8, 12.

9

Satisfying the Client

A consultant's job isn't just to do the work that needs to be done. It's to satisfy the client. Having strong technical skills and the knowledge and ability to carry out the task at hand is important, but technical skills alone are no guarantee of success if the consultant doesn't also know how to relate well with clients. Consulting is a "people business," and just as a doctor strives to develop a good bedside manner, the consultant must work hard to develop good communication skills and to build positive relationships with clients.

The easier and more pleasant it is to work with you, the greater the client's satisfaction level is going to be. Many people picture a consultant as being a lone wolf or a hired gun, someone who comes in, does the job, and then leaves without interacting with the client or the client's staff. In actuality, though, consultants must be able to work with all types of people and must be able to fit into various job situations with ease. In many instances today, consultants work alongside employees at client-companies and become part of the client's team. This is especially true in the area of management consulting. Where once it was enough to offer advice and submit a report, now consultants are often expected to help implement the needed changes, showing how to put their suggestions into practice.

Thus from the moment you first make contact with the client until long after the assignment is completed, you need to focus on ways to better serve the client and to strengthen your working relationship.

KEY ELEMENTS OF CLIENT SATISFACTION

When it comes to explaining what it takes to satisfy them, many clients are like the art patron who says, "I don't know much about art, but I know what I like." Pinpointing what makes a relationship work or what makes it sour isn't always possible. In general, though, there are seven key elements that contribute to client satisfaction:

- Work quality
- Completion time
- Cost
- Communication
- Flexibility
- Dependability
- Attitude

Work Quality

At the core of any consulting assignment is the work itself: what gets done and how. Is the work appropriate? Is it done correctly? Does it meet the client's expectations? Unfortunately, some consultants talk a great game and are good at winning assignments but come up short when it's time to follow through. If you really want to satisfy clients, it's important to do all that you promise . . . and more. This means maintaining high standards of professionalism and performance, employing only those workers and subcontractors who share your commitment to excellence, and using materials and equipment that are suited for the purpose. Bear in mind, too, that the measure of a job's quality is its value to the client. Thus it's critical for you to be able to assess accurately what it is the client truly wants, seeing past the client's stated needs to the needs that are unexpressed or unidentified.

Completion Time

Philosophers and artists may have all the time in the world to develop their visions, but consultants need to keep an eye on the clock. Sticking to schedules and meeting deadlines are part of the job. One of the major causes of client dissatisfaction is not having work completed when it's supposed to be: the consulting assignment that goes on forever with no end in sight. To keep clients' nerves from fraying and your relationships intact, it's essential to complete assignments on time (or early, if possible) and to provide clients with regular progress reports. In the event that you can't meet a deadline, you should notify the client as soon as possible, explaining the situation and discussing what can be done to turn it around. It's critical to keep the client informed and to demonstrate that you're actively taking steps to remedy the problem.

Cost

Nothing can strain a relationship more than when a client feels that he or she is being charged too much. Extreme examples of this include bills for 25-hour days, nonexistent staff members, clerical workers billed as consultants, and $2-per-page photocopying charges. More often than not, though, the real cause of the problem isn't overbilling, but lack of information. Consulting fees and billing procedures must be clarified from the outset. Hourly rates, administrative charges, client-related expenses, and the like should be specified and explained. There is no room for ambiguity here— and never assume. Just because previous clients never questioned certain expenditures doesn't mean that the next client will be so accepting.

The best way to handle disputes over costs is to avoid them in the first place by being candid with clients about what to expect and providing them with itemized bills that document your time and charges. Showing concern for each client's financial situation and doing your best to keep costs down and work within established budget guidelines will also enhance your relationships.

Communication

Like any other relationship, the consultant-client relationship is dependent on communication: two-way communication that flows from you to the client and from the client to you. To satisfy the client and avoid mishaps and misunderstandings, you must be able to share ideas and information. Each of you must know what the other is doing and be working toward compatible goals. Clients often complain that consultants are difficult to contact or don't return their calls promptly. It's crucial for clients to be able to reach you when they need to and to get straightforward answers to their questions. If you travel a lot or have an international practice, take special measures to ensure that clients have access to you. Designating preset reporting times to bring clients up-to-date on your activities, monitoring your messages (phone, fax, and computer), and providing clients with your itinerary can all help to keep the communication lines open.

To serve the client's best interests, it's also important to make sure that you're "in the loop" and are kept informed about matters that affect your duties. For example, legal advisers and public relations consultants are often called after the fact to iron out difficulties or put the right "spin" on a situation when they should have been involved from the beginning. Although it's the client's responsibility to see that you have access to the information you need to do your job properly, not all clients know what to tell a consultant or when to call. Thus one of the ways you can help clients make the best use of your services is by explaining to them the types of information you must have and the various situations in which you should be consulted.

Flexibility

One of the factors that clients often consider in evaluating a relationship is the consultant's flexibility, in terms of both temperament and capabilities. Is the consultant a fast learner? Is he or she open to new ideas? Can the consultant move quickly, adapting to new circumstances and changing direction as needed? Does the consultant have the resources (personnel, equipment, and so on) to devote more time and energy to the assignment if necessary? Because it's not always possible for clients to determine the precise services they need or how big an assignment is going to be, relationships frequently hinge on a consultant's accommodation skills and willingness and ability to do what the situation requires. Consultants who are flexible, adjusting their services and schedules to match their clients' needs, have an edge over those who are not.

Dependability

Although clients look for many things when choosing a consultant—honesty, creativity, technical skills, knowledge, and more—the one thing it takes to keep a relationship going is dependability. Clients need to know that they can count on you. Not only are you going to come through for them on one occasion, but on each and every assignment that you perform. With their futures and fortunes often at stake, clients can't afford to work with a consultant who is undependable. To sustain a relationship, you must be able to convince clients that you are capable of providing reliable service on a regular basis. Unpleasant surprises are out. Continuity and consistency are in.

Attitude

Even if all the other elements are in a consultant's favor, they won't be enough to save a relationship if the consultant has a bad attitude. Consultants who talk down to clients or come across as being arrogant or insensitive are hurting themselves and their businesses. Yet many consultants do just that, either consciously or unconsciously. It may be because they have an inflated sense of their own importance, are covering up for their inadequacies, don't communicate well, or any number of reasons. Whatever the case, clients recognize and resent a poor attitude. Although they may not complain or say anything, once the initial consulting assignment is completed, it's highly unlikely that the consultant will get any repeat business or referrals.

One of the traps to avoid is getting in the habit of thinking of clients as "accounts" or "projects," rather than as individuals who need your help. Clients sense it when a consultant looks at them and just sees dollar signs or thinks of them as another assignment to carry out. The medical specialist who sees a patient as "Monday's gallbladder operation" or "an interesting case" is an example. Intangible as it may be, your attitude toward clients will come through loud and strong, sending a message you may be unaware of or think is unimportant. Your attitude can be a deal maker or a deal breaker, helping or hurting relationships and having a direct impact on your ability to win and keep clients.

BRIDGING THE COMMUNICATION GAP

Among the common complaints raised when clients talk about consultants are these: "I never knew what was going on." "The reports I got were all in jargon." "They came in and acted like they owned the place." "I felt like I was talking to a brick wall." "Considering what I was paying, I don't think it's too much to expect a little courtesy." "I didn't find out there was a problem until it was too late to do anything." "The charges just kept mounting up without any explanation." "The whole thing got out of control." The complaints are different, but each is linked by a single thread: a failure to communicate in a positive way.

Each complaint is an example of people talking *at* each other, rather than *to* each other—or perhaps not talking at all. It's not clear who's at fault—the consultant, the client, or both? What is clear, though, is that in each instance a communication gap exists and is damaging the consultant-client relationship. What makes the situation even worse is that neither party may be aware that there is a communication problem. The client may think that the consultant is rude, inept, or dishonest or is trying to extend the assignment, cover up mistakes, or charge more. The consultant, on the other hand, may think that the client is interfering in the project, trying to steal ideas, or trying to get out of paying for the work performed. In fact, what may really be wrong is that the two parties aren't getting their messages across and expressing themselves in ways that generate a favorable response.

To improve your relations with clients and help keep rifts from occurring, you must bridge the communication gap. The following guidelines—a baker's dozen—is a good place to start.

1. *Treat each person with respect.* People will respond to you better and be more receptive to what you have to say when they know that you hold them in high esteem and recognize the value in who they are or what they have accomplished. The younger you are, the more important it is to show the proper deference to people on the basis of their age or position. A common complaint about management consulting firms is that "they sent me some young MBA right out of school who came in here and tried to tell me how to run my business."

2. *Address people by their names.* Personalizing the work relationship and demonstrating that you know who people are can make all the difference in getting their support. To avoid having this backfire on you, though, find out whether people want to be addressed by their first names or surnames and what titles they prefer (i.e., Miss, Ms., or Mrs., Doctor or Professor, etc.).

3. *Be a good listener.* If you want people to listen to you, you have to learn to listen to them. Don't make the mistake of feeling that you must always be the one doing the talking. It's to your advantage to let clients tell you what they know and to fill you in on the details of their situations. This not only gives you more to go on, but keeps clients involved and interested in what you're doing.

4. *Use positive body language.* Actions *can* speak louder than words. Your facial expressions, posture, and demeanor all have an effect on how people relate to you. Thus it's important to make sure that you

are conveying the right messages and that your body language isn't working against you. Otherwise, you could end up telling the client something entirely different from what you intended. For example, slouching in your chair while reassuring a client that you're committed to meeting a deadline conveys just the opposite message.

5. *Don't underestimate the value of small talk.* Many consultants, especially those in technical fields (science, computing, engineering, and so on), want to talk only about the work itself. Like *Dragnet's* Sergeant Joe Friday ("Just the facts, Ma'am. Nothing but the facts."), they have a very narrow focus. As far as they are concerned, making small talk about people's outside interests, current events, or other topics is a waste of time. Depending on the people you work with, it may be, but a few minutes devoted to small talk can also be time well spent when it comes to cementing a relationship. It can help you and the client develop a better understanding of each other and discover common bonds. In effect, it can open up the relationship and humanize it, adding to your rapport and often leading to future assignments.

6. *Use jargon sparingly.* Every consulting field has its own jargon: the words and phrases used by people within the industry. Jargon serves a real purpose; it tells people specifically what you want to say and demonstrates that you are knowledgeable about your subject. At the same time, though, jargon can also hurt your relationships and distance you from clients if they don't understand it (i.e., "We can double-synch the waves and nex onto the quad or hertz the astrolator effect."). So unless you're absolutely certain that the client knows what you're talking about, you're better off keeping jargon to a minimum or explaining it.

7. *Work within the chain of command.* In your dealings with employees at client-companies, it's important not to overstep your authority. Consultants who come in and start ordering people around without finding out who reports to whom quickly wear out their welcome. To avoid becoming a *persona non grata*, you need to determine ahead of time the scope of your authority and your position in the chain of command: whom you report to and who reports to you.

8. *Don't expect special treatment or privileges.* If you're working alongside the client's employees, you should act and behave as they

do. For example, this means putting money in the coffee kitty from time to time if you're a coffee drinker or making a fresh pot yourself, rather than emptying the pot and expecting someone else to refill it. When employees see that you're willing to chip in and lend a hand, they are more inclined to accept your presence and to assist you in achieving your goals.

9. *Keep the client informed each step of the way.* Providing timely information about your progress will help allay any fears or concerns the client may have. One of the things that bothers clients the most is being left in the dark on a project with no idea of how far along it is or what's been accomplished. The more specific you can be in your reports and conversations, the more comfortable your clients are going to feel.

10. *Give ample warning of any problems you foresee.* If a problem does come up, the worst thing you can do is to spring it on the client. To the extent that it's possible, you should alert the client to potential problems ahead of time and develop strategies for coping with them. By pointing out a problem while it's still on the horizon or in its early stages, you can buy additional time for the client to deal with the situation, and you increase the odds of resolving the problem before it gets out of control.

11. *Explain any fee increases.* If there is an increase in your fees from one bill to the next, it is of vital importance to inform the client and explain why the bill is higher. Rather than just sending out the bill and thinking (or hoping) that the client won't notice the increase, you're better off to point it out yourself and give the reasons behind it: additional costs incurred on the client's behalf, overtime charges, bonus payments, and so on. The same is true if your hourly fees or other charges are going up. In this case, you should give clients advance notice of the new prices and make them aware of what your services will cost in the future. If clients are satisfied with your work, they will usually take reasonable and justifiable fee increases in stride. What they don't like, however, is to have higher-than-anticipated bills summarily presented to them without prior notice.

12. *Provide itemized bills.* Providing clients with itemized bills, rather than just blanket statements of the amounts due, can help bridge the communication gap. In addition to letting clients know what they are paying for, it shows that you are an honest person

with nothing to hide. Although clients may question certain charges or cut back on services that they think are too costly, they will be more inclined to trust you and to continue their relationship with you.

13. *Show that you genuinely care about the client.* The better you are at showing clients through your words and actions that you value your relationships with them and appreciate the opportunity to be of assistance, the more satisfied your clients are going to be. Going out of your way to help when needed, doing something extra without charging for it, and letting clients know about matters that could have an impact on them (changes in the law, new trends, etc.) are just some of the things you can do to underscore that you care about each client's well-being.

GETTING REPEAT BUSINESS AND REFERRALS

If your client relationships are on solid ground, you should have no difficulty getting repeat business or obtaining referrals. Rather than just waiting for additional assignments to come your way, though, there are several measures you can take to speed up the process and to increase your work load. Chapters 5 and 13 look at the things you can do to promote your business and generate additional income. Other measures, specifically related to increasing your repeat business and referrals, include these:

1. *Ask for it.* The first rule of sales is to ask for the order. This applies to repeat sales and referrals too. It's important to let clients know that you are interested in future assignments and are available to carry them out.

2. *Make sure that clients know your capabilities.* Often, clients see a consultant only in narrow terms related to a specific assignment and are unaware of the consultant's full capabilities. By informing clients of the range of services you provide, you can position yourself to get work in other areas.

3. *Identify other needs the client may have.* In the course of carrying out an assignment, you may discover additional areas in which

the client needs help. Bring these to the client's attention with your suggestions for how you can be of assistance.

4. *Offer reduced rates on future work.* To encourage clients to use your services again, you might consider offering them a discount. Because you've already spent time familiarizing yourself with each client's situation and establishing a relationship, your costs associated in taking on other assignments are less, thus justifying the lower rates.

5. *Ask clients if you can use them as a reference.* When soliciting work from prospective clients, it helps to be able to provide them with the names of clients who are already satisfied with your services. As a courtesy, though, and to protect each client's confidentiality, you should never give out a client's name unless you have permission to use it.

6. *Obtain testimonials.* Clients who are pleased with your work may also be willing to write a letter to that effect that you can show to prospects. For additional impact, you might ask them to record their testimonial on audio- or videotape.

7. *Give clients an inducement to make a referral.* Giving clients a gift or a discount on future services in return for telling prospective clients about you is another way to increase your referrals.

8. *Stay in touch with clients.* Contacting clients from time to time after an assignment is completed can also result in additional work or referrals. Your contacts don't have to be official sales calls, but rather updates on what you've each been doing. Following up to make sure the client is satisfied with your work, finding out about the client's current activities, and letting the client know about developments in your industry are all examples of this.

9. *Keep your name in front of clients.* There are numerous things you can do to keep your name uppermost in your clients' minds. As noted in Chapter 5, you can use a variety of networking, advertising, and publicity techniques to accomplish this, ranging from membership in associations to public speaking to brochures and mailings. One of the simplest, most effective ways to ensure that your name is literally in front of your clients (on a desk or close at hand) is to give them advertising specialty items, such as calendars, pens, and notepads, imprinted with your name or logo.

10. *Reciprocate with referrals of your own.* If you encounter people in need of a client's products or services, referring them to the client can benefit both parties while strengthening your ties with the client. From an ethical standpoint, though, you should inform the prospective customer that the business is a client of yours.

10

Handling Ethical Matters

From both a legal and a moral standpoint, consultants must pay attention to the ethical choices they make. Given the positions of trust that they hold, consultants are expected to maintain high ethical standards and act in the best interests of their clients.

Straightforward as this seems—a simple case of "doing the right thing"—when it comes to handling ethical matters, the line between right and wrong, good and bad, isn't always clear-cut. For example, what happens when the interests of one client conflict with those of another or with society's as a whole? What if you're asked to do something that goes against your personal beliefs? What if you have information that the client needs to know—a key employee is quitting, a competitor is bringing out a similar product—but the information was given to you in confidence? What if you stand to gain from the outcome of a recommendation that you make to a client? The decision to tell or not to tell, to perform a task or not to perform it, can involve much soul-searching.

In your role as a consultant, you are likely to face a number of situations in which you must determine the appropriate course of action based on your standards of honesty and integrity. In some instances, there may be laws or regulations that apply or professional guidelines that you can follow, but in others, you will have to rely on personal judgment alone to determine the action to take.

PROBLEM AREAS TO WATCH

Some of the situations in which ethical questions most frequently arise relate to the following consulting issues:

- Confidentiality
- Conflict of interest
- Insider information
- Qualifications
- Performance
- Remuneration
- Personal relationships
- Objectivity
- Loyalty
- Promotion methods

Confidentiality

One thing all successful consultants have in common is the ability to keep a secret. In a business in which information is your stock-in-trade, it is absolutely imperative that you guard confidential information entrusted to you and not disclose it to others. Proprietary information about a client's current work, research or plans, products or processes, personnel, customers and suppliers, contract negotiations, mergers, acquisitions, and sell-offs should, in particular, be closely guarded. Because disclosing this information could damage the client's business or give competitors an unfair advantage, any failure on your part to keep it private could result not only in loss of work, but also in a lawsuit.

Although there is no disputing the need for confidentiality in the consultant-client relationship, numerous ethical questions still come up about the treatment of information and the circumstances under which you may disclose it. Consider the following situations:

- An employee of the client tells you something important "off the record," on the condition that it not be reported.
- You discover information that shows the client's company is operating in a way that is harmful to the environment.
- You know from your work for a previous client that the client you are currently advising is about to make a costly mistake.
- The client confides in you that a much-hyped new product being rushed to market still has some "bugs" in it, but the company doesn't want to miss the key buying season.
- In talking to representatives from one of your client's overseas trading partners, you learn that the client used payoffs to secure the contract with their company.

In each of these situations, you must determine what to tell and to whom, keeping in mind the various factors that apply.

Conflict of Interest

The issue of confidentiality often goes hand in hand with conflict of interest because the latter addresses the question of whose interests come first: those of a past or present client, of the consultant, or of society? Generally speaking, the interests of the client you are currently advising should take precedence over all others' interests. That said, what if protecting a current client's interests means undermining those of a previous client or using information gained while in another client's employ? As you can see, there is a definite conflict that must be resolved. One way to handle it is by refusing to work for the new client because this would jeopardize the position of the previous client. Another way is to accept the assignment but limit your consulting activities to areas in which there are no points of conflict between the two clients' interests. In this instance, both clients should be informed of your work for the other and assured that any confidential information revealed to you will be kept secret.

What about when the conflict is between the client's interests and your own? How do you handle this situation? A common example of this is when consultants perform the dual role of purchasing agent and supplier, recommending specific purchases of goods or services that they then supply the client, such as when

- Computer applications consultants recommend equipment that their firms provide
- Employee training specialists recommend their own firms' books and videos
- Landscape designers also own the nurseries from which the plants and garden supplies for their installations are purchased

In situations like these, it's important for you to let clients know upfront that (1) you stand to benefit from the purchases they make on your recommendations and (2) you will put each client's needs ahead of your own, recommending only the purchases that are in their best interests.

There are other situations in which a conflict of interest may exist between you and the client. For example, you may receive sales commissions from businesses whose goods or services you recommend, or you may have a personal relationship with an owner or employee of a competing company or own shares of stock in the competition. In each of these instances, you should disclose your interests to clients before entering into a consulting agreement with them. If it's determined that the conflict would undermine your ability to serve the client properly, you should not accept the assignment. On the other hand, if the conflict can be resolved (i.e., forgoing the sales commissions or assuring the client that the person you know at the competing company is just a casual acquaintance or that your stock holdings are minimal), it may still be possible for you to proceed as planned.

In dealing with conflict-of-interest issues, disclosure is the key. Clients must be informed of any conflicts that exist (even if it's just the appearance of conflict), and steps should be taken to resolve them before commencing work on an assignment.

Insider Information

Drawing on elements of the first two issues, insider information involves the use of information about a client that is not known to the general public. The most obvious example of this is "insider trading": buying or selling a company's stock based on proprietary information—such as projected earnings, new product development, or expansion activities—that isn't yet available to people outside the company. This practice is not only unethical, but illegal because it gives one group of investors (the insiders) an unfair advantage over other investors (the outsiders). However, if having worked for a client company you then form an opinion about its value as an investment, you have the same right to trade its stock that everyone else does. The ethical question to ask here is, "Are you acting on the basis of your own assessment of the company or on insider information?"

From a legal standpoint, timing is a critical factor. A consultant who makes a big trade in a client's stock the day before key information about the company is released to the public is bound to appear suspect. To avoid even the appearance of insider trading, many consultants make it a practice not to trade shares of stock in the companies they advise. Also, it's not uncommon for companies themselves to stipulate that consultants who work for them must refrain from trading their stock while in their employ.

In deciding how to handle the insider-trading issue, you should consider another factor, in addition to the legal and ethical factors: objectivity. If trading in a company is going to affect your ability to provide the client with an objective viewpoint, that is reason enough not to do it.

Examples of insider information include when a consultant knows about a client's plans and uses this knowledge to obtain additional work or to assist others in obtaining work. In both instances, this may be nothing more than good business sense, keeping one's ear to the ground and capitalizing on an opportunity. On the other hand, if it results in a conflict of interest or involves the disclosure of confidential information then it is unethical.

Qualifications

Tempting as a consulting offer may be, you should never take on an assignment if you lack the necessary skills or experience to carry it out properly. Seeking more challenging assignments that stretch your abilities or enable you to expand your consulting practice is something you can and should do, but misrepresenting your qualifications or promising the client more than you can deliver is not. Rather than claiming to have expertise in an area that you don't, a better approach is to emphasize the expertise that you do have and demonstrate to prospective clients how it can be applied to meet their needs. For instance, a community relations specialist may not have any background in fund-raising but, through his or her work with local groups and businesses, may know how to reach potential donors. That qualification—knowing which people to contact—is the one to stress.

In building your consulting practice, you need to evaluate your qualifications objectively on an ongoing basis to be sure that you can do the things you say you can. Missing out on a coveted assignment can be devastating. What's worse, though, is getting an assignment and then realizing midway through it that you are in over your head and lack the capability to complete it.

Performance

Consultants have a duty to their clients to perform the work contracted for in a timely fashion, providing the highest quality of service that's within their power to provide. This goes without saying, but an ethical question that must often be answered is, Who does the work? Will you carry out the assignment yourself, delegate it to someone in your firm, or subcontract it to an outside consultant? All of these options are acceptable, as long as the client knows who is performing the work and as long as that person is qualified to do it. A problem often occurs when a client thinks the consulting firm itself or one of the principals is doing the work when, in fact, a subcontractor or less experienced junior member is doing it. To avoid this, you should clarify who will be performing the work during the proposal stage of your negotiations with clients. If a client expects you or a specific member of your firm to carry out the assignment, passing it on to someone else would be unethical.

Remuneration

Clients have a right to know what they will pay for the consulting services that you provide. They also have a right to receive itemized accountings of the billable hours or expenses charged to them. Some client companies have gone so far as to demand that consultants working for them provide them with on-line access to billing computers so that they can monitor their consulting fees each day.

To keep remuneration issues from being a problem, it's important for consultants to work out fee and payment schedules in advance and to maintain good accounting records. Even with these precautions, certain ethical matters still need to be considered. For example, how do you itemize an expense if it applies to more than one client? What if part of the time spent on a project was related to your own personal activities? When is an expense reasonable or excessive? When should it be calculated as overhead, and when should it be charged to the client?

Returning to the performance issue, what if an assignment contracted for on a per-project (fixed-fee) basis escalates beyond the original estimates, stretching available resources and cutting into profits? Is it ethical to go back to the client and try to renegotiate the payment terms? Should you cut corners to reduce your costs? Should you transfer the assignment to a consultant with a lower billing rate or subcontract it to an outsider? Or should you bite the bullet and absorb the loss yourself? The answer, in part, depends on your relationship with the client. It also depends on how the decision affects your performance and the quality of the work that the client receives. If the project got out of hand because of extra demands made by the client, you may be justified in seeking a fee increase or billing the client for the additional work. More often than not, though, the best course of action—in terms of ethics and business— is to complete the assignment as promised at the agreed-upon fee. Although you may end up losing money, by demonstrating your honesty and reliability to clients, you will get more work in the future and come out ahead in the long run.

Personal Relationships

Mixing romance with work poses a number of ethical problems. In addition to putting a strain on the consultant-client relationship, it can undermine the consultant's objectivity and make it more difficult to work with members of the client's organization. If a personal relationship does develop, what's the best way to deal with it—with discretion or disclosure? If the person the consultant is involved with is distanced from the consulting project, there's less need to tell the client about the relationship. Conversely, if the person stands to benefit professionally from the relationship or could be perceived as having an undue influence on the project, the client should be informed. Difficult as it may be, the situation can probably be resolved. It's better for the client to hear about the relationship from the consultant than from someone else.

Objectivity

One of the greatest assets a consultant has to offer a client is objectivity: the willingness and ability to look at the client's situation from an unbiased viewpoint and to act in the client's best interests. If, for some reason, you find that you can't be objective, you have a moral obligation to tell the client or to not work on the project. As noted earlier, a consultant's objectivity may be impaired due to a conflict of interest or as a result of a personal relationship. Philosophical differences can also be a contributing factor. For example, a consultant who is adamantly opposed to smoking would have a difficult time working for a tobacco-industry client. So would a conservative Republican political adviser working for a liberal Democratic politician, or an environmentalist for a logging company. In extreme examples such as these, the ethical course of action should be readily apparent. But, what if the philosophical differences are minor or the consultant believes that they can be set aside, keeping personal beliefs and professional behavior separate? This makes it harder to make the right decision.

Loyalty

Determining where your loyalty lies can bring up additional ethical problems. On the surface, the answer seems simple. A consultant's loyalty is to the client—but just who is the client? The person who hires you? That person's boss? The company itself? The board of directors? The shareholders? If everything is going well, it may not matter. On the other hand, what if you find out that the person who hired you is mismanaging his or her department or behaving in a way that could reflect badly on the company? What if the company's resources are being misused or the company is engaged in an illegal activity? What if a member of the board of directors has a conflict of interest? Where does your loyalty lie then, and what should you do? Let someone else deal with the problem? Confront the people involved in it? Go over their heads? Go public with the information? All of a sudden, what seemed simple in the beginning is a lot more complex.

Promotion Methods

An ethical issue that's of special importance to consultants in the legal and medical fields, but that applies to all consultants, is the methods used to promote the business. Obviously, it is wrong to misrepresent a firm's capabilities or to make false or misleading claims about the services provided. Where consultants run into problems is in the gray area between what constitutes reasonable advertising "puffery"—making yourself look good—and an outright lie. In addition to extolling the benefits of using the consultant's services, are prospective clients being adequately warned of the risks? Depending on the type of consulting work you do, there may be specific laws or professional codes of behavior regulating your promotional activities and the means by which you market and sell your services. For example, some professional associations restrict their members from offering gifts, such as free TVs or computer equipment, for using their services because this puts the emphasis on the gift, rather than on the services. Stipulations may also apply to the advertising message or the media used to convey it. With or without restrictions, it is incumbent on all consultants to promote themselves in as honest and factual a way as possible.

DEVELOPING A PERSONAL CODE OF ETHICS

The best way to keep ethical molehills from becoming mountains is to prepare for them by developing a personal code of ethics that you can use to guide your actions and enhance your decision-making ability.

The advantage of having a code of ethics you can refer to is that it can help you to keep ethical issues in perspective and to see how the decisions you make relate to one another. Mapping out the types of ethical conduct that are acceptable or unacceptable to you also gives you more control. Rather than fighting fires and resorting to crisis-management techniques every time an ethical question flares up, you already have established guidelines in place that you can follow.

Given the vital function that a code of ethics serves, it's important to develop your code early in your consulting career, modifying it as needed to reflect your current views and changes in circumstances. A natural starting point is to examine any professional codes of behavior that govern your consulting field. For example, the Association of Consulting Management Engineers (ACME) and the American Society for Training and Development (ASTD) both have detailed codes of ethics that members are expected to abide by in performing their consulting duties. You also need to familiarize yourself with the various laws and regulations that pertain to your profession and the way in which you conduct yourself. Then, building on this, the next step is to incorporate your personal beliefs and values into the mix to create your own code of ethics.

Developing a code of ethics takes time and forces consultants to look closely at their own motivations and intentions, attitudes and behaviors. For these reasons, it's often given a low priority on the things-to-do list. However, by expending the effort to develop a code you can live by, you'll find that you have an invaluable tool to use in shaping your career and building your practice.

Although codes of ethics can vary widely from one profession to the next and from consultant to consultant, certain responsibilities are common to all consultants:

- Accept only the assignments you are qualified to perform.
- Recommend only the services or products that are needed.
- Protect the client's best interests.
- Guard confidential information.
- Establish fair and equitable fees.
- Keep clients informed of your activities.
- Complete assignments in a timely manner.
- Produce high-quality work.
- Uphold the standards of your profession.
- Obey the law.
- Admit mistakes, and work to correct them.
- Promise only the results that you can reasonably achieve.

11

Selling Your Services to the Government

The United States government is the nation's largest customer. In any given year, purchases made by federal, state, and local branches of the government total approximately one-fifth of the gross national product. As pointed out in Chapter 1, among the many things that the government buys are consulting services. The government often does not have the internal resources (time, personnel, expertise, and so on) to achieve its goals. Therefore, if it is to accomplish certain projects, it must rely on outside consultants to perform the necessary tasks.

HOW THE GOVERNMENT OPERATES

Although there are similarities between doing business in the private sector and doing business with the government, there are also distinct differences. For one thing, the government has predetermined purchasing procedures that must be followed. Whereas private businesses are generally free to buy from anyone they choose, the government is required to consider all qualified service providers. Not surprisingly, selling to the government also involves a lot more paperwork than selling to private businesses.

Deciphering the government's abbreviations and jargon; figuring out which person, department, or agency to contact; and complying with the required procedures isn't an easy feat. However, for the consultants who are willing to take the time to learn the system, the rewards can be considerable.

Contracting Procedures

Before awarding a contract, the government usually follows one of two procedures. It issues an Invitation for Bids (IFB) or a Request for Proposals (RFP).

An *Invitation for Bids* states the needs of the procuring agency and defines the work to be done in sufficient detail to permit all bidders to respond to the invitation. Prospective bidders are provided standard forms on which to submit their bids (Figure 11-1), and a specific time for opening the bids is established. If you wish to respond to the IFB, you must submit your sealed bid prior to the bid opening time and must meet the essential requirements of the IFB. Bids that fail to do either of these are considered to be "nonresponsive" and are automatically rejected.

The opening is held in public, and the contract is awarded to the qualified bidder whose bid is the "most advantageous to the government." In other words, *the low bidder gets the contract*. The actual award is usually made within two or three months after the bid opening. This gives the contracting officer time to check all the bids for mistakes and to make sure that the winner is in full compliance with the IFB.

A *Request for Proposals* differs from an Invitation for Bids in that it is less specific regarding the methods that the contractor must employ to carry out the assignment. Although the contracting agency has an idea of the end result that it wants to achieve and the time

Figure 11-1 Solicitation, Offer and Award (Standard Form 33)

SOLICITATION, OFFER AND AWARD	1. THIS CONTRACT IS A RATED ORDER UNDER DPAS (15 CFR 350)		RATING	PAGE OF PAGES

2. CONTRACT NO.	3. SOLICITATION NO.	4. TYPE OF SOLICITATION ☐ SEALED BID (IFB) ☐ NEGOTIATED (RFP)	5. DATE ISSUED	6. REQUISITION/PURCHASE NO.

7. ISSUED BY	CODE	8. ADDRESS OFFER TO *(If other than Item 7)*

NOTE: In sealed bid solicitations "offer" and "offeror" mean "bid" and "bidder".

SOLICITATION

9. Sealed offers in original and _____ copies for furnishing the supplies or services in the schedule will be received at the place specified in Item 8, or if handcarried, in the depository located in _____ until _____ local time _____

(Hour) *(Date)*

CAUTION - LATE Submissions, Modifications, and Withdrawals: See Section L, Provision No. 52.214-7 or 52.215-10. All offers are subject to all terms and conditions contained in this solicitation.

10. FOR INFORMATION CALL:	A. NAME	B. TELEPHONE NO. *(Include area code) (NO COLLECT CALLS)*

11. TABLE OF CONTENTS

(√)	SEC.	DESCRIPTION	PAGES(S)	(√)	SEC.	DESCRIPTION	PAGES(S)
		PART I - THE SCHEDULE				PART II – CONTRACT CLAUSES	
	A	SOLICITATION/CONTRACT FORM			I	CONTRACT CLAUSES	
	B	SUPPLIES OR SERVICES AND PRICES/COSTS				PART III – LISTS OF DOCUMENTS, EXHIBITS AND OTHER ATTACH.	
	C	DESCRIPTION/SPECS./WORK STATEMENT			J	LIST OF ATTACHMENTS	
	D.	PACKAGING AND MARKING				PART IV – REPRESENTATIONNS AND INSTRUCTIONS	
	E	INSPECTION AND ACCEPTANCE			K	REPRESENTATIONS, CERTIFICATIONS AND OTHER STATEMENTS OF OFFERORS	
	F	DELIVERIES OR PERFORMANCE					
	G	CONTRACT ADMINISTRATION DATA			L	INSTRS. CONDS., AND NOTICES TO OFFERORS	
	H	SPECIAL CONTRACT REQUIREMENTS			M	EVALUATION FACTORS FOR AWARD	

OFFER *(Must be fully completed by offeror)*

NOTE: Item 12 does not apply if the solicitation includes the provisions at 52.214-16, Minimum Bid Acceptance Period

12. In compliance with the above, the undersigned agrees, if this offer is accepted within _____ calendar days *(60 calendar days unless a different period is inserted by the offeror)* from the date for receipt of offers specified above, to furnish any or all items upon which prices are offered at the price set opposite each item, delivered at the designated point(s), within the time specified in the schedule.

13. DISCOUNT FOR PROMPT PAYMENT *(See Section I, Clause No. 52.232-8)*	10 CALENDAR DAYS %	20 CALENDAR DAYS %	30 CALENDAR DAYS %	CALENDAR DAYS %

14. ACKNOWLEDGMENT OF AMENDMENTS *(The offeror acknowledges receipt of amendments to the SOLICITATION for offerors and related documents numbered and dated:)*	AMENDMENT NO.	DATE	AMENDMENT NO.	, DATE

15A. NAME AND ADDRESS OF OFFEROR	CODE	FACILITY	16. NAME AND TITLE OF PERSON AUTHORIZED TO SIGN OFFER *(Type or print)*

15B. TELEPHONE NO. *(Include area code)*	15C. CHECK IF REMITTANCE ADDRESS IS ☐ DIFFERENT FROM ABOVE - ENTER SUCH ADDRESS IN SCHEDULE	17. SIGNATURE	18. OFFER DATE

AWARD *(To be completed by Government)*

19. ACCEPTED AS TO ITEMS NUMBERED	20. AMOUNT	21. ACCOUNTING AND APPROPRIATION

22. AUTHORITY FOR USING OTHER THAN FULL AND OPEN COMPETITION ☐ 10 U.S.C. 2304(c)( ) ☐ 41 U.S.C. 253(c)( )	23. SUBMIT INVOICES TO ADDRESS SHOWN IN *(4 copies unless otherwise specified)*	ITEM

24. ADMINISTERED BY *(If other than Item 7)*	CODE	25. PAYMENT WILL BE MADE BY	CODE

26. NAME OF CONTRACTING OFFICER *(Type or print)*	27. UNITED STATES OF AMERICA *(Signature of Contracting Officer)*	28. AWARD DATE

IMPORTANT — Award will be made on this form, or on Standard Form 26, or by other authorized official written notice.

NSN 7540-01-152-8064
PREVIOUS EDITION NOT USABLE

33-134

STANDARD FORM 33 (REV. 4-85)
Prescribed by GSA
FAR (48 CFR) 53.214(c)

Figure 11-1 *(Continued)*

2. **CLEAN AIR AND WATER** *(Applicable if the bid or offer exceeds $100,000, or the contracting officer has determined that orders under an indefinite quantity contract in any year will exceed $100,000, or a facility to be used has been the subject of a conviction under the Clean Air Act (42 U.S.C. 1857c-8(c)(1)) or the Federal Water Pollution Control Act (33 U.S.C. 1319(c)) and is listed by EPA, or is not otherwise exempt.)*
The bidder or offeror certifies as follows:
(a) Any facility to be utilized in the performance of this proposed contract ☐ has, ☐ has not, been listed on the Environmental Protection Agency List of Violating Facilities.
(b) He will promptly notify the contracting officer, prior to award, of the receipt of any communication from the Director, Office of Federal Activities, Environmental Protection Agency, indicating that any facility which he proposes to use for the performance of the contract is under consideration to be listed on the EPA list of Violating Facilities.
(c) He will include substantially this certification, including this paragraph (c), in every non-exempt subcontract.

3. **CERTIFICATION OF INDEPENDENT PRICE DETERMINATION** *(See par. 18 on SF 33-A)*

(a) By submission of this offer, the offeror certifies, and in the case of a joint offer, each party thereto certifies as to its own organization, that in connection with this procurement:
(1) The prices in this offer have been arrived at independently, without consultation, communication, or agreement, for the purpose of restricting competition, as to any matter relating to such prices with any other offeror or with any competitor:
(2) Unless otherwise required by law, the prices which have been quoted in this offer have not been knowingly disclosed by the offeror and will not knowingly be disclosed by the offeror prior to opening in the case of an advertised procurement or prior to award in the case of a negotiated procurement, directly or indirectly to any other offeror or to any competitor; and
(3) No attempt has been made or will be made by the offeror to induce any other person or firm to submit or not to submit an offer for that purpose of restricting competition.
(b) Each person signing this offer certifies that:
(1) He is the person in the offeror's organization responsible within that organization for the decision as to the prices being offered herein and that he has not participated, and will not participate, in any action contrary to (a)(1) through (a)(3), above; or
(2) (i) He is not the person in the offeror's organization responsible within that organization for the decision as to the prices being offered herein but that he has been authorized in writing to act as agent for the persons responsible for such decision in certifying that such persons have not participated and will not participate, in any action contrary to (a)(1) through (a)(3) above, and as their agent does hereby so certify; and (ii) he has not participated, and will not participate, in any action contrary to (a)(1) through (a)(3) above.

4. **CERTIFICATION OF NON-SEGREGATED FACILITIES** *(Applicable to (1) contracts, (2) subcontracts, and (3) agreements with applicants who are themselves performing federally assisted construction contracts, exceeding $10,000 which are not exempt from the provisions of the Equal Opportunity clause.)*
By the submission of the bid, the bidder, offeror, applicant, or subcontractor certifies that he does not maintain or provide for his employees any segregated facilities at any of his establishments, and that he does not permit his employees to perform their services at any location under his control, where segregated facilities are maintained. He certifies further that he will not maintain or provide for his employees any segregated facilities at any of his establishments, and that he will not permit his employees to perform their services at any location, under his control, where segregated facilities are maintained. The bidder, offeror, applicant, or subcontractor agrees that a breach of his certification is a violation of the Equal Opportunity clause in this contract. As used in this certification, the term "segregated facilities" means any waiting rooms, work areas, rest rooms and wash rooms, restaurants and other eating areas, time clocks, locker rooms and other storage or dressing areas, parking lots, drinking fountains, recreation or entertainment areas, transportation, and housing facilities provided for employees which are segregated by explicit directive or are in fact segregated on the basis of race, color, religion or national origin, because of habit, local custom, or otherwise. He further agrees that (except where he has obtained identical certifications from proposed subcontractors for specific time periods) he will obtain identical certifications from proposed subcontractors prior to the award of subcontracts exceeding $10,000 which are not exempt from the provisions of the Equal Opportunity clause; that he will retain such certifications in his files; and that he will forward the following notice to such proposed subcontractors (except where the proposed subcontractors have submitted identical certifications for specific time periods):

Notice to prospective subcontractors of requirement for certifications of non-segregated facilities.

A Certification of Non-segregated Facilities must be submitted prior to the award of a subcontract exceeding $10,000 which is not exempt from the provisions of the Equal Opportunity clause. The certification may be submitted either for each subcontract or for all subcontracts during a period (i.e., quarterly, semiannually, or annually). *NOTE: The penalty for making false offers is prescribed in 18 U.S.C. 1001.*

	AMENDMENT NO	DATE	AMENDMENT NO	DATE
ACKNOWLEDGEMENT OF AMENDMENTS The offeror acknowledges receipt of amendments to the solicitation for offers and related documents numbered and dated as follows:				

NOTE: Offers must set forth full, accurate and complete information as required by this solicitation (including attachments). The penalty for making false statements in offers is prescribed in 18 U.S.C. 1001.

frame for accomplishing that result, it does not have a plan of action to follow. The purpose of the RFP is to gather as many proposals as possible so that the various approaches to carrying out the assignment can be compared. In addition to evaluating each proposal on the basis of its approach, the contracting officer or selection committee takes into consideration the proposer's experience, past performance, personnel, and other resources. Price is still a factor in awarding the contract, but unlike the award of an IFB, being the low bidder is no guarantee that your proposal will be the one selected. Once the evaluation process has been completed, the contract is awarded to the proposer whose offer is considered to be the best.

RFP submissions (which often require the same form as an IFB) are not opened publicly, but must still be received by the established deadline. The winning proposal is sometimes selected without any discussion with the proposer. When this happens, a Notice of Award is sent to the proposer, creating a binding contract. In other instances, discussions or negotiations are necessary before a contract can be awarded. When more than one proposal stands a chance of being selected, all competing proposers must be included in the discussions. These discussions may not disclose any information about a competitor's proposal or price. However, they may indicate any deficiencies in a proposal or if its price is too high. At the conclusion of discussions, all proposers are notified in writing of a date for submission of their final offers. The winning proposal is then selected from those received.

TYPES OF GOVERNMENT CONTRACTS

Government contracts fall into two broad categories: fixed-price contracts and cost-reimbursement contracts. The big difference between the two is that fixed-price contracts require you to perform the agreed-on work at the price that has been set—regardless of what it costs you. Under a cost-reimbursement contract, you are entitled to be reimbursed for your "allowable" costs and to receive a predetermined fee (profit) for your services.

Fixed-Price Contracts

Fixed-price contracts come in several shapes and sizes, including the following variations.

Firm Fixed-Price Contract

This is the most commonly issued type of fixed-price contract. The price is firm for the duration of the contract and is not subject to any adjustments, except for authorized changes. It works best when your costs are reasonably predictable and you can arrive at a price with a high degree of accuracy. A firm fixed-price contract places maximum risk on you, the contractor, because all costs above the set price are your responsibility. On the positive side, if your costs are less than anticipated, your profit will be higher.

Economic Price Adjustment Contract

Some fixed-price contracts contain economic price adjustment clauses that protect you and the government against wide fluctuations in labor or in materials cost when market conditions are unstable. These clauses stipulate that the contract price can be increased or decreased in response to higher or lower costs. The contract will frequently contain a ceiling price that the government will not exceed, no matter what the cost fluctuations may be.

Fixed-Price Redetermination Contract

Under this type of contract, you and the government contracting officer establish an initial price for your services, a ceiling price, and a time for redetermination. At the time of redetermination, you submit a proposal based on your actual costs to date and the estimated cost of any incomplete work. After a government audit, you negotiate a revised price. This price may be higher or lower than the initial price, but it may not exceed the ceiling price.

Fixed-Price Incentive Contract

This type of contract is similar to a redetermination contract. The difference is that an incentive contract contains a target cost and a formula for determining your profit. The formula rewards you with more profit if your actual costs are less than the target cost and takes away profit if your costs exceed the target. As with the redetermination contract, you cannot be paid more than the ceiling price.

Cost-Reimbursement Contracts

The following types of cost-reimbursement contracts represent those most frequently issued by the government.

Cost-plus-Fixed-Fee Contract

This type of contract is issued more often than any of the others in its group. Under it, you and the contracting agency agree on the estimated cost of contract performance and a fixed fee (profit) that you will receive for doing the work. You are entitled to recover all of your allowable costs (as defined in the contract) and your fixed fee. Regardless of whether your actual costs are greater or less than the estimated cost, you still receive the same fee.

Cost-plus-Incentive-Fee Contract

The cost-plus-incentive-fee contract calls for you and the contracting officer to agree on a target cost, a target fee, and an incentive formula for determining your final fee. The formula provides for an adjustment in the fee based on any difference between the target cost and the actual cost. If your costs turn out to be less than the target cost, your fee is increased accordingly. Unlike the fixed-price-incentive contract discussed earlier, this contract doesn't have a price ceiling. However, it does place minimum and maximum limits on the fee adjustment that can be made.

Cost-plus-Award-Fee Contract

In addition to reimbursing you for your costs, this contract provides for the payment of two kinds of fees: a base fee and an award fee. The base fee is set in advance, but the award fee is pegged to the contract officer's evaluation of your performance. The performance areas that are rated include the quality of the work, your timeliness in completing the assignment, the ingenuity shown, and cost effectiveness.

FINDING OUT ABOUT CONTRACT OFFERINGS

Before you can compete for a government contract, you must be aware of the contract offering. You can use all of the following information sources to find out about consulting opportunities with the government.

Bidder's Mailing Lists

One of the best ways to find out about government contracts is to be included on the Bidder's Mailing List (BML) for each government department or agency with whom you wish to do business. This can be accomplished by filling out a Solicitation Mailing List Application (Standard Form 129) and submitting it to the appropriate procurement offices (Figure 11-2). Copies of the form can be obtained from the General Services Administration, described later in the chapter, or directly from the government procurement offices.

Once your name has been placed on a Bidder's Mailing List, IFB and RFP solicitations will automatically be sent to you. To remain on the list, you must respond to each IFB or RFP by (1) submitting a bid or proposal or (2) writing that you are unable to bid on the transaction but wish to remain on the active Bidder's Mailing List. Failure to do either of these may result in your name being removed from the list.

Figure 11-2 Solicitation Mailing List Application (Standard Form 129)

53.301-129   FEDERAL ACQUISITION REGULATION (FAR)

SOLICITATION MAILING LIST APPLICATION	1. TYPE OF APPLICATION ☐ INITIAL ☐ REVISION	2. DATE	FORM APPROVED OMB NO. 9000-0009

NOTE: Please complete all items on this form. Insert N/A in items not applicable. See reverse for instructions.

Public reporting burden for this collection of information is estimated to average .58 hours per response, including the time for reviewing instructions, searching existing data sources, gathering and maintaining the data needed, and completing and reviewing the collection of information, including suggestions for reducing this burden, the FAR Secretariat (VRS), Office of Federal Acquisition Policy, GSA, Washington, DC 20405; and to the Office of Management and Budget, Paperwork Reduction Project (9000-0002), Washington, DC 20503.

3. NAME AND ADDRESS OF FEDERAL AGENCY TO WHICH FORM IS SUBMITTED (Include Zip Code)	4. NAME AND ADDRESS OF APPLICANT (Include county and Zip code)

5. TYPE OF ORGANIZATION (check one) ☐ INDIVIDUAL ☐ NON-PROFIT ORGANIZATION ☐ PARTNERSHIP ☐ CORPORATION, INCORPORATED UNDER THE LAWS OF THE STATE OF:	6. ADDRESS TO WHICH SOLICATIONS ARE TO BE MAILED (If different than item 4)

7. NAMES OF OFFICERS, OWNERS, OR PARTNERS

A. PRESIDENT	B. VICE PRESIDENT	C. SECRETARY
D. TREASURER	E. OWNERS OR PARTNERS	

8. AFFILIATES OF APPLICANT (Names, locations and nature of affiliation. See definitions on reverse.)

9. PERSONS AUTHORIZED TO SIGN OFFERS AND CONTRACTS IN YOUR NAME (Indicate if agent)

NAME	OFFICIAL CAPACITY	TELE. NO (Include area code)

10. IDENTIFY EQUIPMENT, SUPPLIES, AND/OR SERVICES ON WHICH YOU DESIRE TO MAKE AN OFFER (See attached federal agency's supplemental listing and instructions, if any.)

11A. SIZE OF BUSINESS (See definitions on reverse) ☐ SMALL BUSINESS (If checked, complete items 11B and 11C) ☐ OTHER THAN SMALL BUSINESS	11B. AVERAGE NUMBER OF EMPLOYEES (Including affiliates) FOR FOUR PRECEDING CALENDAR QUARTERS	11C. AVERAGE ANNUAL SALES OR RECEIPTS FOR PRECEDING THREE FISCAL YEARS $

12. TYPE OF OWNERSHIP (See definitions on reverse) (Not applicable for other than small business) ☐ DISADVANTAGED BUSINESS ☐ WOMAN-OWNED BUSINESS	13. TYPE OF BUSINESS (See definitions on reverse) ☐ MANUFACTURER OR PRODUCER ☐ REGULAR DEALER (Type 1) ☐ CONSTRUCTION CONCERN ☐ SURPLUS DEALER ☐ SERVICE ESTABLISHMENT ☐ REGULAR DEALER (Type 2) ☐ RESEARCH AND DEVELOPMENT

14. DUNS NO. (If available)	15. HOW LONG IN PRESENT BUSINESS?

16. FLOOR SPACE (Square feet)		17. NET WORTH	
A. MANUFACTURING	B. WAREHOUSE	A. DATE	B. AMOUNT $

18. SECURITY CLEARANCE (If applicable, check highest clearance authorized)

FOR	TOP SECRET	SECRET	CONFIDENTIAL	C. NAMES OF AGENCIES WHICH GRANTED SECURITY CLEARANCES (Include dates)
A. KEY PERSONNEL				
B. PLANT ONLY				

CERTIFICATION - I certify that information supplied herein (including all pages attached is correct and that neither the applicant nor any person (or concern) in any connection with the applicant as a principal or officer, so far as is known, is now debarred or otherwise declared ineligible by any agency of the Federal Government from making offers for furnishing materials, supplies, or services to the Government or any agency thereof.

19. NAME AND TITLE OF PERSON AUTHORIZED TO SIGN (Type or print)	20. SIGNATURE	21. DATE SIGNED

NSN 7540-01-152-8086 Previous edition usable	EXPIRATION DATE: 9-30-91 129-107	STANDARD FORM 129 (REV. 6-90) Prescribed by GSA - FAR (48 CFR) 53.214(c)

Figure 11-2 *(Continued)*

INSTRUCTIONS

Persons or concerns wishing to be added to a particular agency's bidder's mailing list for supplies or services shall file this properly completed and certified Solicitation Mailing List Application, together with such other lists as may be attached to this application form, with each procurement office of the Federal agency with which they desire to do business. If a Federal agency has attached a Supplemental Commodity list with instructions, complete the application as instructed. Otherwise, identify in Item 10 the equipment, supplies, and/or services on which you desire to bid. (Provide Federal Supply Class or Standard Industrial Classification codes, if available) The application shall be submitted and signed by the principal as distinguished from an agent, however constituted.

After placement on the bidder's mailing list of an agency, your failure to respond (submission of bid, or notice in writing, that you are unable to bid on that particular transaction but wish to remain on the active bidder's mailing list for that particular item) to solicitations will be understood by the agency to indicate lack of interest and concurrence in the removal of your name from the purchasing activity's solicitation mailing list for the items concerned.

SIZE OF BUSINESS DEFINITIONS
(See Item 11A.)

a. Small business concern—A small business concern for the purpose of Government procurement is a concern, including its affiliates, which is independently owned and operated, is not dominant in the field of operation in which it is competing for Government contracts and can further qualify under the criteria concerning number of employees, average annual receipts, or other criteria, as prescribed by the Small Business Administration. (See Code of Federal Regulations, Title 13, Part 121, as amended, which contains detailed industry definitions and related procedures.)

b. Affiliates—Business concerns are affiliates of each other when either directly or indirectly (i) one concern controls or has the power to control the other, or (ii) a third party controls or has the power to control both. In determining whether concerns are independently owned and operated and whether or not affiliation exists, consideration is given to all appropriate factors including common ownership, common management, and contractual relationship. (See Items 8 and 11A.)

c. Number of employees—(Item 11B) In connection with the determination of small business status, "number of employees" means the average employment of any concern, including the employees of its domestic and foreign affiliates, based on the number of persons employed on a full-time, part-time, temporary, or other basis during each of the pay periods of the preceding 12 months. If a concern has not been in existence for 12 months, "number of employees" means the average employment of such concern and its affiliates during the period that such concern has been in existence based on the number of persons employed during each of the pay periods of the period that such concern has been in business.

TYPE OF OWNERSHIP DEFINITIONS
(See Item 12.)

a. "Disadvantaged business concern"—means any business concern (1) which is at least 51 percent owned by one or more socially and economically disadvantaged individuals; or, in the case of any publicly owned business, at least 51 percent of the stock of which is owned by one or more socially and economically disadvantaged individuals; and (2) whose management and daily business operations are controlled by one or more of such individuals.

b. "Women-owned business"—means a business that is at least 51 percent owned by a woman or women who are U.S. citizens and who also control and operate the business.

TYPE OF BUSINESS DEFINITIONS
(See Item 13.)

a. Manufacturer or producer—means a person (or concern) owning, operating, or maintaining a store, warehouse, or other establishment that produces, on the premises, the materials, supplies, articles, or equipment of the general character of those listed in Item 10, or in the Federal Agency's Supplemental Commodity List, if attached.

b. Service establishment—means a concern (or person) which owns, operates, or maintains any type of business which is principally engaged in the furnishing of nonpersonal services, such as (but not limited to) repairing, cleaning, redecorating, or rental of personal property, including the furnishing of necessary repair parts or other supplies as part of the services performed.

c. Regular dealer (Type 1)—means a person (or concern) who owns, operates, or maintains a store, warehouse, or other establishment in which the materials, supplies, articles, or equipment of the general character listed in Item 10, or in the Federal Agency's Supplemental Commodity List, are bought, kept in stock, and sold to the public in the usual course of business.

d. Regular dealer (Type 2)—In the case of supplies of particular kinds (at present, petroleum, lumber and timber products, machine tools, raw cotton, green coffee, hay, grain, feed, or straw, agricultural liming materials, tea, raw or unmanufactured cotton linters and used ADPE), Regular dealer means a person (or concern) satisfying the requirements of the regulations (Code of Federal Regulations, Title 41, 50-201.101(a)(2) as amended from time to time, prescribed by the Secretary of Labor under the Walsh-Healey Public Contracts Act (Title 41 U.S. Code 35-45). For coal dealers see Code of Federal Regulations, Title 41, 50-201.604(a).

• COMMERCE BUSINESS DAILY—The Commerce Business Daily, published by the Department of Commerce, contains information concerning proposed procurements, sales, and contract awards. For further information concerning this publication, contact your local Commerce Field Office.

STANDARD FORM 129 BACK (REV. 6-90)

Government Agencies

Both the General Services Administration and the Small Business Administration provide individuals and firms with detailed information about obtaining government contracts.

The *General Services Administration* (GSA) serves as the purchasing agent for the federal government. It is responsible for buying most of the products and services used by federal departments and agencies. To help businesses understand how the government's procurement system works, the GSA has established GSA Business Service Centers in several major cities. The business experts in these centers can provide you with the following:

- Detailed information about contracting opportunities, including those that have been set aside for small and disadvantaged businesses
- Bidder's Mailing List applications
- Copies of bid abstracts, indicating prices bid and who the successful bidders were
- Publications designed to assist business representatives in doing business with the government

Figure 11-3 lists the addresses and phone numbers of the GSA Business Service Centers.

The *Small Business Administration* (SBA) wants to see that small businesses receive their fair share of government contracts. To accomplish this, the SBA works closely with government agencies to develop procurement policies and procedures that will increase the number of contracts awarded to small-business concerns. SBA procurement center representatives (PCRs) are stationed at all federal installations, both military and civilian, that have major buying programs. The PCR's job is to make sure that small businesses are not being excluded from the contracting process and to try to obtain small-business set-asides whenever possible. Competition for contracts designated as small-business set-asides is restricted to small businesses; large businesses are not permitted to submit bids or proposals.

In addition to helping small businesses win government contracts, the SBA helps them win subcontracting assignments by working

Figure 11–3 GSA Business Centers

General Services Administration
Business Service Centers

Central Office
Director of Public Services
18th and F St. N.W.
Washington, DC 20405
202-708-5082

Region 1: New England
Regional Director of Business Affairs
General Services Administration
John W. McCormick Post Office and Courthouse
Boston, MA 02109
617-565-8100

Region 2: New Jersey, New York, Puerto Rico, and the Virgin Islands
Regional Director of Business Affairs
General Services Administration
26 Federal Plaza
New York, NY 10007
212-264-1234

Region 3: Mid-Atlantic
Regional Director of Business Affairs
General Services Administration
Ninth and Market St.
Philadelphia, PA 19107
215-656-5515

Region 4: South
Regional Director of Business Affairs
General Services Administration
1776 Peachtree St. N.W.
Atlanta, GA 30309
404-331-5103

Figure 11–3 *(Continued)*

Region 5: Great Lakes
Regional Director of Business Affairs
General Services Administration
230 Dearborn St.
Chicago, IL 60604
312-353-5383

Region 6: Missouri Valley
Regional Director of Business Affairs
General Services Administration
1500 E. Bannister Rd.
Kansas City, MO 64131
816-926-7203

Region 7: Southwest
Regional Director of Business Affairs
General Services Administration
819 Taylor St.
Fort Worth, TX 76102
817-334-3284

Region 8: Upper Midwest and Mountain
Regional Director of Business Affairs
General Services Administration
Building 41
Denver Federal Center
Denver, CO 80225
303-236-7408

Region 9: California, Hawaii, and Nevada
Regional Director of Business Affairs
General Services Administration
525 Market St.
San Francisco, CA 94105
415-744-5050

Figure 11–3 *(Continued)*

Region 9: California, Hawaii, and Nevada—continued
Regional Director of Business Affairs
General Services Administration
300 N. Los Angeles St.
Los Angeles, CA 90012
213-894-3210

Region 10: Northwest and Alaska
Regional Director of Business Affairs
General Services Administration
440 Federal Building
915 Second Ave.
Seattle, WA 98174
206-931-7956

---

with prime contractors to ensure that they use qualified small businesses as subcontractors on government projects. In this regard, SBA subcontracting specialists regularly visit large government contractors and make the capabilities of small businesses known to them.

To facilitate the matchup between small businesses and the government agencies and major contractors who can benefit from their services, the SBA has developed the Procurement Automated Source System (PASS). PASS is designed to provide agencies and contractors with profiles of small businesses who are potential bidders on contracts or subcontracts. By having your consulting firm listed on the PASS computerized roster, you can broaden your exposure and gain valuable information about contract offerings. To be included in PASS, all you need to do is fill out a Company Profile form and mail it back to the SBA (Figure 11-4). Copies of the form can be obtained from SBA field offices. (See Chapter 15 for the addresses.)

Figure 11–4 PASS Company Profile Form

Increase your business opportunities!
List your company in SBA's Automated
Directory of Small Businesses...PASS

Complete and Return this Form To:
U.S. Small Business Administration
P.O. BOX 9000
Melbourne, FL 32902-9919

SBA
PASS

Instructions:	Complete all items on this form as accurately as possible. Key items are defined on the reverse side of the form. The form must be signed by a principal of the company as distinguished from an agent, however constituted. The completed form will constitute official self certification as to size, minority, and/or woman owned status. See certification statement at signature block. Write N/A in boxes if not applicable.
What Happens:	We will notify you as soon as your company is listed in the Procurement Automated Source System (PASS). Your company's capabilities are then available to many Government agencies and major corporations when they request potential bidders for contracts and subcontracts. Remember - although PASS increases your exposure, it does NOT guarantee solicitations or contracts. PASS should be just one element of your regular marketing efforts.
PASS is Free!	You have nothing to lose and possibly new contracts to gain. Don't delay...Return this applicatiion today!

The following company profile is ☐ a new listing or ☐ an updated listing.

PROCUREMENT AUTOMATED SOURCE SYSTEM (PASS) - COMPANY PROFILE

Identification Section

Company Name_____

Mailing Address_____

City_____ State _____ ZIP _____

Phone Number ( )   -   FAX Number ( )   -

Contact _____ Title _____

Employer Id Number_____
(EIN, Tax Id, or SS#)
DUNS Number_____
(DUN & Bradstreet)
Year Business Established_____
Average Gross Revenues_____
(Last Three Years)
Average Number of Employees_____
(Last Twelve Months)

Organizational Data

Type of Organization - ☐ Corporation   ☐ S. Corporation   ☐ Sole Proprietorship   ☐ Partnership

Parent Company Name_____
Average Gross Revenue (Last Three Years)_____
Average No. Employees (Last Twelve Months)_____

Affiliate Name_____
Average Gross Revenue (Last Three Years)_____
Average No. Employees (Last Twelve Months)_____

Affiliate Name_____
Average Gross Revenue (Last Three Years)_____
Average No. Employees (Last Twelve Months)_____

Affiliate Name_____
Average Gross Revenue (Last Three Years)_____
Average No. Employees (Last Twelve Months)_____

Ownership Data

Check boxes appropriately if company is at least 51% owned, controlled and actively managed by any of the following. (Note: Minority Person includes Black, Hispanic, Native American, Asian Indian, or Asian Pacific)

☐ U.S. Citizen ☐ Minority Person ☐ Woman/Women ☐ Veteran ☐ Disabled Veteran ☐ Vietnam Vet. (1964-1975)

If you checked Minority Person, check one of the following.

☐ Black American ☐ Hispanic American ☐ Native American ☐ Subcontinent Asian American ☐ Asian Pacific American

Native American includes American Indian, Eskimo, Aleut, and Hawaiian - Subcontinent Asian American includes India, Pakistan, Bangladesh, etc.* - Asian Pacific American includes Orientals, Pacific Islands, Philippines, etc.*   *For complete list, refer to 13 CFR 124.105b

Business Types

PASS is divided into 4 types of business. Please estimate the percentage of your business allocated to the following (total must equal 100) and complete the appropriate Section(s).

Manufacturing/Supplies ☐ %

Check Applicable Box(es)

☐ Manufacturer ☐ Dealer ☐ Wholesale Distributor

Manufacturing Facility Size_____SQ. FT.

Construction ☐ %

Current Aggregate Bonding Level $_____
Current Bonding Level Per Contract $_____
Maximum Operating Radius_____(miles)
-Anywhere in the U.S., enter 3999 above.
-Anywhere in the World, enter 9999 above.

Research and Development ☐ %

Number of Engineers and Scientists_____
Expertise of Key Personnel (Limit 150 Characters)_____
_____
_____

Services ☐ %

Current Aggregate Bonding Level $_____
Current Bonding Level Per Contract $_____
Maximum Operating Radius_____(miles)
-Anywhere in the U.S., enter 3999 above.
-Anywhere in the World, enter 9999 above.

Figure 11–4 *(Continued)*

Capabilities Section *(Limit 350 characters; be concise and avoid abbreviations and generalities)*

List products, services, special capabilities, and important categories under which you want your business listed. The system searches businesses based on the capabilities you list in this section.

Standard Industrial Classification (SIC) Code(s)

If unknown, leave blank. Appropriate codes will be assigned.

Special Equipment/Materials *(Limit 50 characters)*

List

CAGE Code	Manufacturing Quality Assurance	Miscellaneous
	☐ MIL-I-45208 ☐ MIL-Q-9858 ☐ Other _____	Metric Capability ☐ Yes ☐ No Accept VISA Credit Card ☐ Yes ☐ No

Security Clearance

	Top Secret	Secret	Confidential	Other
Key Personnel	☐	☐	☐	☐
Site	☐	☐	☐	☐

If other provide description _____

Export Activity

☐ Active Experienced Exporter
☐ Interested And/Or New to Exporting
☐ Not Interested

If you checked Active or Interested, please check one or more of the following geographic areas.

☐ Western Europe   ☐ Middle East
☐ Eastern Europe/NIS   ☐ Asian Pacific
☐ The Americas   ☐ Africa

Performance History (Contract References)

Contract Start Date _____	Contract Start Date _____
Dollar Value _____	Dollar Value _____
Product/Service Desc. _____	Product/Service Desc. _____
Contact Name _____	Contact Name _____
Contact Phone No. _____	Contact Phone No. _____
Contract Start Date _____	Contract Start Date _____
Dollar Value _____	Dollar Value _____
Product/Service Desc. _____	Product/Service Desc. _____
Contact Name _____	Contact Name _____
Contact Phone No. _____	Contact Phone No. _____

Definitions

SIZE OF BUSINESS - A small business concern for the purpose of Government procurement is a concern, including its affiliates, which is independently owned and operated, is not dominant in the field of operation in which it is competing for government contracts and can further qualify under the criteria concerning number of employees, average annual receipts, and other criteria as prescribed by the U.S. Small Business Administration. (See Code of Federal Regulations, Title 13, Part 121, as appended, which contains detailed industry definitions and related procedures.)

MINORITY/WOMEN/VETERAN OWNED STATUS - Qualifying firms must be at least 51% owned, controlled, and actively managed by such individuals.

CAGE Code (Commercial and Government Entity Code) This is a code assigned to contractors providing goods and services to the Federal Government. For information about CAGE codes, call (616) 961-4955

DISASTER RESPONSE - Firm's capacity for disaster response (if any) should be included in the capability statement. Required information includes 24 hour-a-day contact and the ability to ship manufactured goods within 24 hours of receiving order.

QUALITY ASSURANCE - Information applies to manufacturing processes for the Department of Defense.

CERTIFICATION - I certify 1) that this is a small business as defined in the DEFINITION section; 2) that the characteristics of the firms ownership are accurately reflected in the OWNERSHIP section; 3) that all information supplied herein (including all attachments) is correct; and 4) that neither the applicant nor any person (or concern) in any connection with the applicant as principal or officer, so far as known, is now debarred or otherwise declared ineligible by any agency of the Federal Government from making offers for furnishing materials, supplies, or services to the Government or any agency thereof.

INFORMATION IN THIS PROFILE MAY BE DISCLOSED AT THE DISCRETION OF THE U.S. SMALL BUSINESS ADMINISTRATION

Signature of Company Officer _____ Title _____ Date _____

Please Note: The estimated burden hours for the completion of this form is 15 minutes per response. If you have any questions or comments concerning this estimate or any other aspect of this information collection please contact, Chief Administrative Information Branch, U.S. Small Business Administration, 409 3rd St., SW, Washington, D.C. 20416, or Gary Waxman, Clearance Officer, Paperwork Reduction Project (3245-0024), Office of Management and Budget, Washington, D.C. 20503

SBA Form 1167 (3/93)
OMB Approved: 3245-0024 Exp: (3/31/96)
*U.S. GPO: 1993-358-240/89139

Government Publications

Each of the following government publications can provide you with additional information about selling your consulting services to the government.

- *Commerce Business Daily.* This publication is published Monday through Friday by the Department of Commerce. It lists civilian agency and military procurement invitations, subcontracting leads, contract awards, sales of surplus property, and foreign business opportunities. If you are serious about doing business with the government, this publication is a must. Copies are available at SBA field offices, GSA Business Service Centers, and many public libraries. Subscriptions can be obtained through the Superintendent of Documents, Government Printing Office, Washington, DC 20402. You can also obtain *Commerce Business Daily* via your computer through CBD Online.
- *Federal Acquisition Regulation.* To make sure that you fully understand the government's policies and procedures on granting contracts, this publication, which is also available on CD-ROM, can keep you informed of the latest rules and regulations. The basic manual, with supplements or quarterly updated discs, is available through the Government Printing Office.
- *How to Sell to the United States Department of Commerce.* Designed to help potential government contractors, this booklet discusses the mission and functions of the Department of Commerce, what it buys, and how to get started in government contracting. Copies are available through the Government Printing Office.
- *Selling to the Military.* In this publication, you can obtain addresses and telephone numbers of major buying offices of the army, navy, air force, and Defense Logistics Agency. It summarizes the procurement responsibilities and purchases of each office and gives advice on how to make your capabilities known. The publication is for sale by the Superintendent of Documents, Government Printing Office,

or may be obtained from Department of Defense contracting offices.

- *Selling to the U.S. Government.* This publication explains government buying methods, how to locate purchasing agencies, what they buy, how to have an opportunity to bid on government contracts, and how to prepare bids and proposals. It is available free of charge from the Small Business Administration.
- *U.S. Government Purchasing and Sales Directory.* This directory provides a listing of products and services bought by all federal agencies, keyed to the purchasing offices that buy them. You can obtain it from the Small Business Administration.

Public Notices

Another way that the government informs potential bidders of contract offerings is through public notices. These notices are often placed in newspapers, trade and professional publications, and government bulletins released by various agencies. Notices are also sent to individuals who have expressed an interest in being considered for specific types of contracts.

TIPS FOR SELLING YOUR SERVICES

1. Determine which government agencies are most likely to need the type of consulting services you can provide.
2. Focus your selling efforts on the best prospects, securing placement on each agency's Bidder's Mailing List.
3. List your consulting firm on the SBA's PASS roster so that government agencies and contractors can be made aware of your capabilities.
4. Respond to each Invitation for Bids or Request for Proposals that you receive, thereby maintaining your status on the corresponding Bidder's Mailing Lists. (Note: Your response must be in writing.)

5. Increase your success rate by making sure that your bids or proposals meet the requirements of each IFB or RFP.
6. Don't overlook subcontracting opportunities; once a major contract has been awarded, contact the winning consulting firm to express your interest in working on the assignment.
7. Get to know the contracting officers of the various departments and agencies; whenever possible, visit their offices regularly.

12

Going International

More and more consultants are going international. Lured by the opportunity to expand their client bases, increase profits, and work on challenging projects, consultants from a wide spectrum of industries are looking abroad. Once the province of a few megafirms with telex addresses after their names, international consulting is now attracting small and medium-size businesses, too. Helped in part by major advances in transportation and communication systems that make it easier to do business around the globe, even solo practitioners are discovering that they can make the world their marketplace.

Entering foreign markets isn't without its risks. Overcoming the barriers of time and distance is just the beginning. You must also learn to adapt to different economic, political, legal, and cultural environments. Client needs, wants, beliefs, and behaviors can vary widely from one country to the next, and a consultant who fails to take this into consideration is asking for trouble. For example, a negotiating tactic or sales technique that works in one country may be offensive in a second country and illegal in a third. Thus, in setting your sights overseas, it's important to do your market research first and to develop a game plan you can follow.

ASSESSING THE GLOBAL MARKETPLACE

When deciding whether to pursue consulting opportunities outside the United States, you should evaluate your current situation, taking into account your capabilities and objectives, and determine which foreign markets have the greatest demand for your services. When looking at where you stand, for instance, you should weigh factors like these:

- Your current workload
- The time constraints on you
- Your strengths and weaknesses
- Your willingness to travel
- The resources at your disposal
- How efficiently you are meeting existing clients' needs
- What new challenges you seek
- What sets you apart from other consulting firms
- How you could apply your expertise in other countries
- Your ability to adapt to a foreign environment

Developing an international consulting practice requires stamina and commitment. To balance the needs of domestic and foreign clients, you have to be able to juggle schedules, conform to local preferences and practices, and get the maximum value out of your resources. Good organizational skills are a must, along with a talent for interacting with people from diverse backgrounds.

Having looked closely at your situation, if you believe that going international would be to your advantage, the next step is to decide which foreign markets to enter. Inasmuch as even the biggest consulting firms can't be in every country at once, it's essential to choose your target markets carefully, pinpointing the countries that offer the greatest profit potential. When assessing each country, ask yourself the following:

- How big is the market for my services?
- Is the market growing or shrinking?
- Which organizations or individuals are likely prospects?
- What level of revenues could I reasonably generate? At what cost?
- Who would my competitors be?
- What government regulations or restrictions would have an impact on me?
- What kind of infrastructure (roads, water, electricity, transportation, communication) is in place?
- What technology is available?
- How difficult would it be to contact prospective clients?
- Are there local support services (legal, advertising, personnel, etc.) that I can use?
- How stable are the political and economic systems?
- Is the country safe?
- Would I feel comfortable doing business there?

Look for an Environmental Fit

As you're evaluating what each country has to offer, you should be looking for an environmental fit: a matchup between the things you need to function effectively as a consultant and what the country is able to provide. The better equipped a potential "host country" is to accommodate your requirements, the easier it will be for you to gain entry to the market and to conduct your business there. For instance, you may find that some countries are inhospitable due to their strict licensing requirements, high costs, or taxes. Other countries may not have adequate technological facilities or support services to enable you to do your work, or the level of competition could be so high that the market is already saturated.

In your search for countries that have the environmental fit you need to operate your consulting business, it's important not to lose sight of your priorities. What factors are most critical to your success? Which are negotiable? Which are not? For example, if access to a high-speed supercomputer is essential to your work, that is a key factor to consider. For you to pursue your goals and objectives profitably, the environments in which you choose to work must be capable of sustaining your type of consulting business. Keep in mind, too, that an appropriate country for one consultant may not be right for another consultant whose priorities are different. Finding the right environmental fit means finding the fit that's right for you.

Put Marketing Research Data to Use

To get the answers to your questions and assess accurately the foreign demand for your consulting services, you should make use of the array of marketing research data that's available. The following are among the most common sources of marketing information:

- The U.S. government
- Foreign governments
- International organizations
- Trade and professional associations
- International banks and investment houses
- American chambers of commerce abroad
- Publications, software, and databases

The U.S. Government

The U.S. government can provide a wealth of information about doing business overseas. Following are some of the departments and agencies that focus on international marketing issues.

Department of Commerce.   Established to support and promote the commercial activities of American business both within the United States and abroad, the Department of Commerce (DOC) keeps close tabs on the international marketplace and is an excellent source of information. Specific agencies within the DOC that concentrate on foreign trade include the International Trade Administration, U.S. and Foreign Commercial Service, and the Center for International Research. Each of these agencies has trade specialists available to answer questions and provide assistance to consultants seeking to enter foreign markets or to compete more effectively in them. In addition, they can provide general economic and statistical data on a country-by-country basis as well as customized reports that are individually tailored to your needs.

Small Business Administration.   Like the Department of Commerce, the Small Business Administration exists to provide advice and assistance to businesses. Through its Office of International Trade, the SBA provides counseling, training, and advice on identifying which foreign markets to enter, contacting foreign business representatives, and complying with local laws.

Department of State.   Through its Bureau of Economic and Business Affairs and representatives stationed in U.S. embassies and consulates around the world, the Department of State (DOS) is able to obtain up-to-the-minute information about developments in foreign countries. As a result, DOS officers can be of particular help in gauging local economic and political conditions and in dealing with operational matters related to foreign trade policies.

Foreign Governments

The governments of the countries you are seeking to enter or in which you are already doing business are another important source of information. You can either contact the governments overseas or their representatives in the United States. The commercial attaches assigned to foreign embassies and consulates can be particularly helpful not just in providing research data about their countries, but in providing business leads and introductions and helping you cut through bureaucratic red tape.

International Organizations

A number of international organizations collect country-by-country data that may be of use to you. Organizations that are actively involved in gathering business-related information include the following.

United Nations.   The major source of world economic data, the United Nations is dedicated not only to preserving international peace, but to maintaining an environment that is favorable to economic cooperation and world trade. Toward this end, it conducts studies on world and regional economic developments and publishes many reports and reference books of interest to consultants working in foreign countries. United Nations publications that are especially good sources of international marketing research are the *Statistical Yearbook*, the *International Trade Statistics Yearbook*, and the *Demographic Yearbook*.

Organization of Economic Cooperation and Development.   This organization, which represents many of the world's leading industrialized nations, compiles monthly statistics on foreign trade flows from country to country as well as detailed economic surveys on each member nation's production and employment levels, changes in prices and wages, and so on.

World Bank.   Established in 1945 to promote economic and social progress in developing nations by providing advice and access to investment capital, the World Bank is an excellent source of data on business activity, productivity levels, and growth rates. In addition, it's a good clearinghouse of information on contracting opportunities available to U.S. businesses.

Trade and Professional Associations

Trade and professional associations representing specific industry or service areas, such as the oil industry or the structural engineering field, are often gold mines of information about foreign markets. Better still, they provide a means of networking with other consultants and industry leaders and of making contact with prospective clients. For more information on associations and the benefits available through them, see Chapter 15.

International Banks and Investment Houses

The international departments of commercial banks and investment houses can also be of help to consultants. Providing information and services through branch offices within the United States and abroad, they can assist you in finding foreign lenders or investors, running credit checks on potential clients, assessing local market conditions, determining exchange rates, and so on.

American Chambers of Commerce Abroad

Branches of the chamber of commerce located in cities around the world are especially good sources of information on local market conditions and the day-to-day realities of doing business abroad. Set up for the purpose of promoting business interests, they are often in a position to provide business leads, introductions, and referrals.

Publications, Software, and Databases

Much of the information you need to assess the global marketplace and develop your game plan should be readily available in print or via computer programs and on-line databases. Following are examples of the information sources at your disposal:

Publications
Breaking into the Trade Game, U.S. Small Business Administration, Washington, DC.
Business America, U.S. Government Printing Office, Washington, DC. Published biweekly, the purpose of this publication is to help U.S. businesses compete more effectively overseas by providing them with information and analysis on foreign markets and world trade developments.
Developing Your International Business Plan, Lake Michigan College, International Business Center, Benton Harbor, MI.
International Business, American International Publishing Corporation, New York. This monthly publication focuses on current de-

velopments in international trade and the global marketing environment.

The World Is Your Market, by Clark C. Cassell, Braddock Communications, Washington, DC.

Software and Databases

International Business Network, American International Publishing Company, New York. On-line network for international business research.

National Trade Data Bank, U.S. Department of Commerce, Washington, DC. CD-ROM disc released monthly that provides updated information on international trade activity and country-specific developments.

PC Globe, Michigan Small Business Development Center, Wayne State University, Detroit. Software program on world demographics and geographic information.

Drawing on these information sources, combined with your own personal observations and experience, you should be well equipped to determine which foreign markets look the most promising.

BREAKING INTO THE MARKET

Once you've identified the countries in which you would like to do business, there are a number of things that you can do to break into the market. Unlike manufacturers and retailers, you don't have to line up production facilities or distributors. Thus, your primary concern is making contact with prospective clients. As noted in Chapter 5, it's important to develop an overall communication strategy that enables you to reach prospective clients and keep them informed of the types of consulting services you have to offer. In addition to the promotion methods already described, the following methods are among those that work best on an international level:

- Expositions and trade fairs
- International conventions and professional meetings

- Personal introductions
- Trade opportunities program leads
- Matchmaker events
- Trade missions
- ITA catalog and video exhibitions

Expositions and Trade Fairs

One of the best means of introducing and promoting your services in foreign markets is through expositions and trade fairs, where you're able to meet prospective clients face to face. This offers you the opportunity to see many people at once as well as to size up the competition. To get the most out of expositions and trade fairs, make sure that you participate in ones that will draw the types of clients you've identified in your target market. You should also have any brochures or other materials you intend to give out printed in the language of the country hosting the event. The location of your booth can be critical, too. In choosing a location, look at a diagram of the site where the event is being held to determine where you will be positioned. The closer you are to the front entrance and main aisles, the better.

To find out about upcoming expositions and trade fairs in various countries, you can contact the U.S. and Foreign Commercial Service branch of the Department of Commerce or look for the annual schedule of events published in *Business America* magazine. Gale Research also has a book entitled *Trade Shows Worldwide*, which lists the dates and locations of upcoming shows.

International Conventions and Professional Meetings

Conventions, professional meetings, and symposia are another excellent means of making yourself known. In addition to meeting other consultants in your field and exchanging information on the latest industry developments, you're likely to come into contact with prospective clients who have come to hear what the speakers and panelists have to say.

Personal Introductions

To make contact with prospective clients, never underestimate the power of a personal introduction. Arranging for someone you know to introduce you to a prospect not only enables you to reach a decision maker, but comes with the seal of approval of the person who makes the introduction. Thus, when devising your strategy for breaking into foreign markets, it's important to think of the people you know who might be able to assist you: friends and relatives, colleagues, former employers or professors, clients. Perhaps someone you've met at a trade fair or convention will be willing to help.

In many countries, especially those in which networking is the primary means of promotion, an introduction is essential for making contact. One person introduces you to another person who introduces you to the person you want to meet. The introduction may take place in a business setting or, more often than not, at an informal gathering or party in someone's home. Be forewarned, though, when using foreign intermediaries. Your go-betweens may expect to be paid for their introductions. If you aren't careful, you could run afoul of the U.S. Foreign Corrupt Practices Act. What's viewed by one person as a tip or reasonable fee for services rendered may be viewed by another person as a bribe, which is illegal. Given these circumstances, it's important to talk to an attorney before you agree to make payments to foreign intermediaries who offer to assist you.

Trade Opportunities Program Leads

One way to obtain introductions to the people you need to meet is by utilizing the International Trade Administration's (ITA) Trade Opportunities Program (TOP). ITA officers in countries around the world gather leads daily of foreign customers seeking specific products and services. These leads, including name and contact information, are then made available to U.S. businesses through the Department of Commerce and through newspapers, trade publications, and computer bulletin boards.

Matchmaker Events

The Department of Commerce also organizes "matchmaker events" in which American businesses seeking to expand overseas are matched with prospective foreign clients for their goods or services. The DOC then schedules trips to the various countries where the matchmaker events are held and brings the parties together. Each trip generally lasts a week or less and the DOC coordinates the transportation, facilities, itinerary, official receptions, and so on.

Trade Missions

Similar to matchmaker events, trade missions are trips organized around a specific theme or industry, such as world ecology or the automobile industry. They often involve seminars and discussions designed to improve trade relations between the nations represented. Trade missions can be especially helpful when it comes to increasing your visibility as an expert in your field or meeting local business and government representatives who might otherwise be difficult to reach.

ITA Catalog and Video Exhibitions

If the time and expense associated with participating in a matchmaker event or trade mission are too much for you, you might want to take advantage of an International Trade Administration Catalog and Video Exhibition instead. A low-cost, easy alternative to taking your show on the road, the ITA Catalog and Video Exhibitions do it for you, showcasing your promotional literature or video presentation to qualified prospects in foreign markets around the world. Department of Commerce officers overseas monitor the response to your business and forward any leads to you. On the average, a participant can expect to receive 50 qualified leads.

OVERCOMING CULTURAL BARRIERS

When doing business overseas, one of the biggest challenges you're likely to face is learning how to adapt to each country's culture. Even if you speak the language of the people you'll be interacting with, there are still numerous cultural barriers to overcome due to national differences in manners, traditions, values, beliefs, and attitudes.

What's socially acceptable in one country or setting may be a blatant faux pas in another. Something as simple as shaking hands or keeping an appointment can be fraught with peril. In the first instance, do you shake hands or not? If so, how firm a grip should you use? Americans generally favor a strong handshake, Europeans favor a lighter one, and the Japanese would just as soon not shake hands at all. As for keeping appointments, do you arrive early, on time, or a few minutes late? Once you've arrived, do you get right down to business or engage in small talk? It all depends on where you are. In countries where time is viewed as being linear, with each minute ticking inexorably away, not to be repeated, punctuality is the norm, as evidenced by such sayings as "Time is money," "Time waits for no man," and "The early bird gets the worm." On the other hand, in countries where time is viewed as being cyclical, repeating itself like the changing seasons, there's less concern for sticking to set schedules.

High-Context versus Low-Context Cultures

In your dealings with clients, you should also be aware of the fact that it's not just what you say that's important, but how you say it. In high-context cultures, such as those found in much of Asia and the Middle East, nonverbal communication—facial expressions, eye contact, glances, posture, gestures, and other movements—often carry more weight than the actual words that are spoken. Conversely, in low-context cultures, like that of the United States, the word is the thing, and what is said is more likely to be taken at face value. These differences in context—high and low—often lead to cultural conflicts and misunderstandings. For example, Americans—who are viewed as straight-forward, plain-speaking, get-to-the-point businesspeople at home—can easily be seen as pushy, disrespectful, or untrustworthy abroad.

Negotiation Techniques

One of the times when culture clash is most likely to occur is during negotiations. This isn't surprising when you consider that you and the client are not only in close proximity to each other, but may be working at cross-purposes as you each seek to obtain the best terms for yourselves.

To avoid personal conflicts and enhance your effectiveness as a negotiator, keep the following guidelines in mind:

1. **Learn as much as you can about each country in which you are doing business.** You should have a general understanding of the local customs and behaviors. To help familiarize yourself with other cultures, we highly recommend the book *Do's and Taboos Around the World* by Roger Axtell (John Wiley & Sons).
2. **If you don't speak the client's language, bring an interpreter.** Don't assume that the client will speak your language or will provide an interpreter for you.
3. **Let the client set the pace.** As noted before, getting right down to business in one country may be a virtue, whereas in another country it's looked on as being rude.
4. **If more than one person is present during negotiations, try to determine each person's role.** Pay special attention to each person's rank and position, and show the proper deference to each participant in the negotiations.
5. **Remember the nonverbal messages you are sending.** Be particularly careful about how you sit and the types of gestures you use. For example, if you cross your legs, make sure that the bottom of your shoe—which is often viewed as unclean—isn't facing the client. You'd also be wise to avoid making the "okay" gesture (thumb and forefinger joined in

a circle) because in many countries it's considered to be obscene.

6. **Be patient.** Remember that time is relative and what seems to be taking forever to you may be the normal course of events.

7. **Don't be intimidated by silence.** Silence during negotiations is to be expected. Rather than being a sign of disinterest or rejection, it can mean that the client is seriously thinking about your offer or wants you to elaborate on it. In fact, knowing that it makes Americans uncomfortable, some foreign negotiators will use silence to their advantage to get a better offer.

8. **Take a long-term approach.** Don't just think of the initial deal or a single consulting project. Through your negotiation efforts, let clients know that you are interested in building a long-term relationship. This is especially important in a country like Japan, where business relationships can span centuries, evolving from one generation to the next.

In general, you'll find that people around the world are more similar than they are different. Although their customs and behaviors may vary, when it comes to choosing a consultant, they want someone who can provide the expertise and services they need and who will put their interests first. By showing that you are that person and taking the time to learn about prospective clients' cultures and environments, you should be able to overcome any obstacles that you encounter in going international.

13

Generating Additional Income

In addition to the basic consulting services that you provide, there are a number of other ways to market your knowledge and expertise. Speaking, conducting seminars, writing articles, publishing newsletters, and producing training materials are just a few of the ways you can earn additional income. In some instances, the income generated by these "fringe" activities can even exceed income from consulting activities.

SOURCES OF INCOME

Each of the activities or products discussed below represents another source of income that is available to consultants.

Selling Supplies or Merchandise

One of the most logical and lucrative ways that consultants can generate additional income is through the sale of related supplies

163

and merchandise. Interior designers and space planners, for example, often obtain the furnishings and fixtures that are required for a project, then charge the client for the purchase cost plus a percentage markup. Security systems consultants not only advise clients on how to guard against intruders and prevent property losses, but also provide them with the security devices to do the job. A physical-fitness consultant might market a line of exercise equipment or sportswear. Time-management consultants can sell datebooks, calendars, and forms specifically designed to aid clients and others in implementing their time-management techniques.

Developing Computer Programs

Computer programs that enable customers to have instant access to a consultant's decision-making ability or other skills have become a steadily growing source of income for many consultants. Even if you are not in a computer-related field, you may still be able to use this method to package your knowledge by working with a computer software designer to develop programs that will meet the needs of your intended customers. For instance, a financial planner might sell a program that analyzes stocks for investors. A marketing consultant might create a program that identifies sales trends.

Public Speaking

Public speaking is a way to enhance both your bank balance and your reputation. Experts in such diverse fields as human relations, inventory control, taxes, entrepreneurship, communications, stress management, and personal selling are finding ready audiences for their presentations. Noncelebrity speakers are routinely paid between $500 and $2,500 to deliver a one-hour talk at a luncheon or dinner meeting. Celebrities who are already well known to their audiences can earn upwards of $25,000. Along with the speaking fee and expenses that you receive, there's the opportunity to come into contact with prospective clients.

Launching yourself as a professional speaker isn't as difficult as you might think. You can do it through your own promotional efforts or through the services of a lecture bureau, which will handle bookings for you in exchange for 30 to 40 percent of your fee. If you opt to do it yourself, the following suggestions should help you get started:

1. Build up your confidence and hone your speaking skills by volunteering to speak for free in the beginning.
2. Contact the program chairpeople of the local business and civic organizations whose members are most likely to benefit from your information. The Rotary Club, Business and Professional Women's Club, Chamber of Commerce, Kiwanis, and similar groups all have ongoing needs for speakers.
3. Describe the talk that you are prepared to give, and offer to speak at an upcoming meeting.
4. Make audiotapes of your speeches so that you can evaluate them later. They can also be used as audition tapes.
5. Get in touch with the producers of local radio and television talk shows that reach the people you want to reach, and let them know that you have information that might be of interest to their audiences. This can be done via the telephone, but you should follow it up by sending a letter and your resume.
6. Put together a brochure that describes your background and the various topics on which you are qualified to speak.
7. List yourself in one or more speakers' directories that program chairpeople and corporate executives use to select speakers.

Once you've developed your presentation and gained some experience in speaking to an audience, you are ready to go after paid speaking engagements. Your best prospects include trade and professional associations, corporations, convention bureaus, unions, and government agencies.

To locate lecture bureaus that represent speakers in your particular field, look in the yellow pages under "Lecture Bureaus" or "Booking Agents." For more information, contact the following:

National Speakers Association
5201 N. Seventh St.
Phoenix, AZ 85014

International Platform Association
2564 Berkshire Rd.
Cleveland Heights, OH 44106

Giving Seminars

Another way to generate additional income is by conducting seminars. Instead of waiting to be invited to speak at a luncheon or dinner meeting, you can plan and promote your own event. In this case, you handle all of the arrangements, from finding an appropriate location in which to hold the seminar to sending out direct-mail brochures or placing ads in local newspapers.

The Seminar Format

Depending on its topic, audience, and price, a seminar can last anywhere from three hours to one or more days. You may be the sole presenter or one member of a panel of guest speakers. Some seminars are structured so that participants have a maximum opportunity for interaction with the seminar leader; others are structured more like lectures with a question-and-answer session at the end. Refreshments are optional. The most elaborate formats call for coffee and sweet rolls in the morning, lunch during the afternoon break, and beverage service throughout the day. For evening seminars or those lasting less than four hours, it isn't necessary to serve refreshments, although coffee and ice water are always welcome.

Facilities and Costs

There are a number of locations in which you can hold seminars—for instance, hotels, conference centers, auditoriums, colleges and universities, public buildings, community meeting rooms in shopping malls, banks, churches, even department stores (in conjunction with a special promotion). Some creative seminar planners even offer their seminars on cruise ships and airplanes. Based on the number of participants who will be attending the seminar, you might be able to hold it in your office or home. One publishing consultant holds a three-part series of evening seminars in her penthouse apartment and serves wine and cheese to the participants.

The cost to stage and promote a seminar can range from less than $500 to more than $10,000. Several factors will determine your total cost:

- Facility rental cost
- Refreshment cost
- Materials cost
- Promotion cost

You should be able to rent an average-size meeting room (one that seats up to 50 people) for somewhere between $50 and $250 per day. A larger room or auditorium will be more expensive. Hotels and conference centers frequently provide free meeting space if you order a certain number of lunches or dinners. They make their profits from the meal service rather than from the facility rental.

Some hotels provide beverage service (coffee and ice water) at no extra charge, including it in the price of the meeting room. Others price it separately, charging $5 to $10 each pot of coffee that you serve and a flat fee of $10 for ice water. If you provide lunch or dinner as part of the seminar, you'll probably spend between $10 and $30 per person. The items on the menu and the type of meal service you choose (sit-down or buffet) will largely determine the cost.

You must also ask yourself what seminar materials or handouts the participants will receive. The costs of producing any workbooks, audio- or videotapes, kits, supplies, or other materials you plan to give participants must be included in your total cost. Some consultants keep their costs low by limiting each handout to just a few pages. Others provide attractively bound workbooks and packaged sets of audiotapes. Generally, you should wait until you have successfully conducted enough seminars to know the participants' needs before investing the time and money to create elaborate materials.

Promotion is likely to comprise the largest expenditure of your total seminar cost. The two most widely used methods of seminar promotion are direct-mail and newspaper advertising, used separately or in combination. For the best results, it pays to know your target market. The more accurately you can pinpoint which prospects will be the most receptive to your seminar offering, the better your response will be. Once you have identified your best prospects, you can determine which media to use and what advertising message will be the most effective. When your best prospects are concentrated in a particular industry, group, occupation, or other category, direct mail tends to be the most effective means of reaching them. Its high degree of selectivity enables you to get your advertising materials into the right hands. If you are trying to reach a diverse audience that is less easily identifiable (such as people in need of financial advice), newspaper advertising is the best method to use. For more information on promotion techniques, see Chapter 5.

Seminar Fees

Your seminar fee must be high enough to cover your costs and provide a sufficient amount of profit. A three-hour seminar can cost the participant anywhere from $25 to $150, and an all-day seminar can run from $100 to $450. One way to determine a fee is to set a goal for the total revenues you wish to generate from the seminar. Then divide that figure by the estimated number of people who will attend the seminar. The result is the fee you need to charge. If the seminar fee seems too high in comparison with the competition, you can try either to attract more participants or to lower your revenue goal, thereby reducing your fee.

Teaching

Your professional experience and academic background may qualify you to teach classes at the college or university level. Community colleges, state colleges and universities, and private schools often augment their full-time teaching staffs with part-time instructors who are knowledgeable in specialized fields. From the school's point of view, hiring outsiders on a part-time basis keeps instructional costs low and gives students access to teachers with current, first-hand experience in their fields of expertise. This arrangement is also advantageous from the part-time teacher's point of view. In addition to being a personally satisfying experience, teaching (1) adds professional credibility, (2) provides an opportunity to polish speaking and presentation skills, and (3) creates additional income.

The prerequisites for becoming a part-time instructor vary from state to state and from one school to another. Depending on the subject area, a master's degree and two years' professional experience alone may be sufficient. When it comes to teaching classes in vocational studies and fine arts, the emphasis is usually on professional experience. Other departments, such as English, history, math, and science, place greater emphasis on academic credentials. Part-time instructors' salaries, which are generally set at an hourly rate, range from $25 to $60 per hour.

Selling Audiotapes

Another means of packaging and presenting your knowledge is through audiotapes. They can be sold in conjunction with speaking engagements and seminars or by direct mail. Audiotapes are particularly appealing to salespeople and business executives who are on the road a lot and want to make productive use of their driving time. The greatest demand is for self-help tapes on such subjects as time management, positive thinking, selling techniques, communication skills, and real estate investments.

A major advantage of selling audiotapes is their high profit margin. A single 60-minute tape typically sells for $15 to $20. A package of four to eight tapes can sell for $60 to $150 or more. The actual unit cost is usually only a small fraction of the sales price. The larger your order, the lower your unit costs will be. To locate production studios in your area, check the yellow pages under "Audiovisual Production Services" or "Tapes."

Selling Videotapes

Many consultants who have been successful in marketing seminars and audiotapes are now turning to videotapes as an alternative medium for reaching their audiences. In this way, the purchaser of the tape can *see* your presentation, viewing it as often as desired at his or her convenience. Although a videotape is considerably more expensive to produce than an audiotape, it also fetches a much higher sales price. A 30-minute videotape generally sells for anywhere from $40 to $300. The simpler your video production is, the less it will cost. A one-camera setup, in which you are the sole actor and only a few special effects are used, will be less expensive than a three-camera setup with several actors, different sets, and numerous special effects. For more details about producing videotapes, contact the production studios in your area. You should also check with the television stations (local and cable); they often lease out their production facilities and crews.

Writing Articles

More than 50,000 newspapers and magazines are currently published in the United States. These numbers include daily and weekly newspapers and consumer and trade magazines. Given the need to provide their readers with the most up-to-date and thorough information available, the majority of these publications accept articles written by free-lance writers. Depending on the topic and the writer's reputation, a two-thousand-word article can sell for between $200 and $2,000.

When it comes to selecting a topic, writing experts generally advise that you write about something you know. Thus, a marketing consultant might choose to write about such topics as these:

Advertising	Pricing
Brand names	Product development
Consumer behavior	Shipping methods
Distribution	Trends and fashions
Packaging	

Any one of these topics could result in a wealth of articles directed at marketing professionals or the general public. For instance, the topic "advertising" might yield these articles:

- "How Advertisers Convince You to Buy"
- "Subliminal Selling — Does It Work?"
- "Tailoring Your Ads to the Foreign Market"
- "Choosing an Ad Agency"
- "Measuring the Effectiveness of Your Ads"
- "What the Ads Don't Tell You"
- "Madison Avenue Imagemakers"
- "Advertising Jingles Keep Cash Registers Ringing"
- "TV Networks Vie for Advertisers' Dollars"
- "How Susceptible Are You to Advertising?"

Before you sit down and begin to write an article, it's a good idea to spend some time thinking about who will publish it. Rather than writing an article and sending the finished manuscript to prospective publishers, it's usually better to send a query letter first. A query letter describes the article you intend to write and explains why it will be of interest to the publication's readers. It should also highlight your qualifications, emphasizing that you have the background and experience to write the proposed article.

From the editor's point of view, there are two advantages to receiving a query letter over a manuscript: (1) A query letter can be read quickly, and (2) if the idea appeals to the editor, he or she can work with the writer to develop the right approach for the article. From the writer's point of view, the advantages are that (1) it takes less time to write a query letter than to write an entire article, (2) a query letter stands a better chance of being read (unsolicited manuscripts are often returned unopened), and (3) editors usually respond more quickly to query letters.

Once you've sold an editor on your idea, you can proceed to write the article, tailoring it to meet the needs of the publication in which it will appear.

To give your finished manuscript a professional appearance, be sure to follow these guidelines:

1. Type it neatly on 8.5-by-11-inch white paper (20-pound weight).
2. Type the title of your article in the upper left-hand corner of the first page. On separate lines below this, type your name, address, phone number, and the length of the manuscript (number of words).
3. Start the first line of copy approximately one-third of the way down the first page.
4. Double-space your manuscript, leaving a one-inch margin on all sides of the page.
5. Number each page (except the first) in the upper right-hand corner; along with the number, put your last name and a shortened form of the title. ("How Advertisers Convince You to Buy" might be written "Advertisers Convince.")
6. Type one of the following notations on the last page of your manuscript below the last line of copy: ###, -30-, or The End. This lets the editor know that there is no additional material to follow.
7. Use a paper clip, rather than a staple, to hold your manuscript pages together; this is more convenient for the editor.

Once your article is ready to send out to a newspaper or magazine, prepare a *cover letter* to go with it. Your cover letter should set forth your reasons for submitting the article to the publication, why the article is of value, and the professional background that qualifies you to write it. If you previously sent a query letter to the publication and were told to go ahead and write the article, make a note of this in your cover letter ("Per your request, enclosed is my article, 'How Advertisers Convince You to Buy.' As you may recall from the query letter I sent you in June, this article is about . . .").

Last but not least, don't forget to enclose a self-addressed, stamped envelope (SASE) with your manuscript. This will ensure its safe return to you if, for some reason, the publication is unable to use it. Some writers feel that enclosing an SASE is inviting failure by assuming from the start that the manuscript will be rejected. This isn't the case. Enclosing an SASE shows that you have a professional approach toward your writing and are aware of the rules of publishing etiquette.

Publishing Reports

Another way to combine your consulting expertise and writing talents is by publishing reports. A report can be anywhere from a few pages in length to more than a hundred, held together by a staple or presented in an attractive binder. Its purpose is to convey current information that will enable the purchaser of the report to take a course of action. For instance, an insurance consultant might prepare a 40-page report aimed at the owners and managers of medium-size businesses. Entitled "How to Keep Your Company's Insurance Costs Down," it would provide the reader with a step-by-step plan for setting up an improved program of risk management. A real estate consultant could put together a 15-page report, "Your Dream House—How to Find It, How to Buy It," designed to help prospective home buyers make the right decisions.

The price that a customer is willing to pay for a report depends on how badly he or she wants the information. The quality and the relevance of the information are what counts, not the number of pages. You can charge more for a 20-page report on a high-interest subject than for an 80-page report on a low-interest subject. Generally, you should be able to sell a 20-page report for $25 to $100. If the information is particularly timely or would be difficult to obtain by other means, your price could be considerably higher.

Publishing Newsletters

One source of income that seems ideally suited to consultants is newsletter publishing. Like consultants' services, newsletters provide clients with information and assistance on an ongoing basis. Newsletters might inform readers about the changes occurring in a particular field or might advise what steps they should take to accomplish specific goals. By gathering information from a variety of news sources (the media, industry leaders, bankers, stock analysts, and so on) and condensing it into a few pages, newsletters save the reader time. By drawing attention to key facts or interpreting the reasons behind recent developments, newsletters help the reader make decisions.

The more frequently you publish your newsletter, the more time-consuming and costly it will be to produce. Some newsletters are published weekly; others on a biweekly, monthly, or quarterly basis. In the beginning at least, you should stick to a monthly or quarterly schedule. Later, after you've learned a few publishing shortcuts, you can increase the frequency of issues if the demand warrants it. Another factor to consider is the size of your newsletter. This can range from two pages (one 8.5-by-11-inch sheet of paper printed on both sides) to more than 20 pages. The most common size for a newsletter is four pages (one 8.5-by-17-inch sheet of paper printed on both sides and folded in half).

Newsletter prices, like report prices, are determined by how valuable their information is to readers. Some newsletters cost as little as $15 for a one-year subscription, while others cost $1,000 or more. Those in the latter category include a few investment newsletters as well as newsletters whose primary subscribers are corporations.

Writing Books

One of the most satisfying ways to generate additional income is by writing books. Along with the financial rewards and professional recognition that you can derive from writing books, they provide an opportunity to present readers with an in-depth view of the subject.

There are two basic methods for getting your book published: (1) You can sell it to an independent publishing house in much the same way as you would sell an article, or (2) you can publish it yourself. If you choose the first method, you will have the benefit of the publishing house's editorial and marketing expertise, and you won't have to invest your own money to produce the book. At the same time, though, you won't have control over the price of the book or how it is promoted. The second method, known as *self-publishing*, gives you the greatest degree of control, but it also entails the most risk. In addition to financing the publishing project yourself, you must find someone to typeset the book (or do it yourself with a desktop publishing program) and a printer to print and bind the copies. Then it's up to you to market the book using such means as direct mail, book wholesalers, seminars, and the like.

To find out more about writing and publishing, we recommend that you read the following publications:

Books

How to Get Happily Published: A Complete and Candid Guide by Judith Appelbaum, Harper Reference, New York.

How to Publish, Promote and Sell Your Own Book by Robert Lawrence Holt, St. Martin's Press, New York.

Literary Market Place, R. R. Bowker, New York, annual. Lists magazines, newspapers, book clubs, agents, reviewers, and a variety of related services.

Publishers, Distributors and Wholesalers of the United States, R. R. Bowker, New York, annual. Lists major publishers, distributors, wholesalers, small presses, associations that act as publishers, and software publishers.

The Self-Publishing Manual: How to Write, Print and Sell Your Own Book, Para Publishing, P.O. Box 8206-240, Santa Barbara, CA 93118-8206.

Ulrich's International Periodicals Directory, R. R. Bowker, New York, annual. Lists thousands of periodicals.

Working Press of the Nation, National Research Bureau, Burlington, IO, annual. Lists newspapers, magazines, feature writers, editors, and addresses.

Writer's Market, Writer's Digest, Cincinnati, OH, annual. Lists the places where you can sell any kind of writing: articles, nonfiction books, novels, short stories, scripts, and more. It gives the names and addresses of editors, how much they are paying, and what their editorial needs are.

Magazines

Publishers Weekly, 249 W. 17th St., New York, NY 10011.
Writer's Digest, 1507 Dana Ave., Cincinnati, OH 45207.

14

Record Keeping and Taxes

As an independent consultant, it is essential for you to maintain good financial records. The most obvious reason for this is that the more accurate and up-to-date your records are, the easier it will be to prepare your income tax returns. There are other reasons, as well. Along with the need to keep good records to satisfy the government, you also need them for your own benefit. Setting up an efficient record-keeping system is the best way to ensure that you receive all of the business-related tax deductions to which you are entitled. It should also go a long way toward pleasing your clients because you will have fewer billing errors. In addition, by helping you to recognize problems or opportunities quickly, your records can be a valuable tool in making business decisions. Good records enable you to substitute facts for guesswork, continuity for confusion. Instead of having to hunt for the financial information you need or develop it on the spot, you already have it in hand, ready to be used.

INFORMATION YOUR RECORDS SHOULD PROVIDE

Your record-keeping system should include the following information:

- Monthly income totals
- Business operating expenses
- Accounts receivable totals
- Financial obligations coming due
- Current sources of income
- Services or products most in demand
- Your best clients
- Clients behind on their bills
- Money invested in supplies and inventory
- Total value of your assets
- Overall profitability

This information, which is necessary for tax reporting and management purposes, is also likely to be required by lending institutions, suppliers, and others with whom you do business.

CHOOSING A RECORD-KEEPING SYSTEM

The Internal Revenue Service does not stipulate what kind of records a business owner must keep, only that the records properly document the business's income, expenses, and deductions. Thus, you may use any record-keeping system that meets this criterion and is suited to your consulting practice. For best results, the system you choose should be (1) simple to use, (2) easy to understand, (3) accurate, (4) consistent, and (5) capable of providing timely information.

You can choose from among a number of business record-keeping systems, ranging from the traditional double-entry system used by accountants to the simpler single-entry and pegboard systems available at stationery and business-forms stores.

Double-Entry Record-keeping System

The double-entry record-keeping system is the most difficult to use of the various systems, but because of its built-in checks and balances, it provides the greatest degree of accuracy. At the same time, it has the capacity to provide a greater amount of financial information than the other systems. Based on the balance sheet for your business, it requires you to make two entries for every transaction that you record because all transactions involve an exchange of one thing for another. For instance, if a client pays cash for an audiotape or other merchandise that you sell, the amount of money in your consulting practice increases while your inventory level decreases. Under the double-entry system, you must record both changes in your books: one as a debit entry and the other as a credit entry. This is where the checks and balances come in. For each transaction, the total debit amount must always equal the total credit amount. If the amounts are out of balance, the transaction has been improperly recorded.

Single-Entry Record-keeping System

The single-entry record-keeping system differs from the double-entry system in that it is based on your income statement, rather than your balance sheet. In this respect, it doesn't require you to "balance the books" or record more than one entry for each transaction. The simplicity of the system is its best feature and what makes it so appealing to the owners of new or small businesses. For tax purposes, the system enables you quickly and easily to record the flow of income and expenses generated by your consulting practice. In addition to this, a good single-entry record-keeping system provides a means of keeping track of your accounts receivable, accounts payable, depreciable assets, and inventory. An accountant or bookkeeper can set up a system specially tailored to the needs of your practice, or you may find that one of the commercially available, ready-made systems meets your requirements. Generally consisting of worksheets bound together in a spiral notebook, these systems can be purchased at office-supply and stationery stores. The most popular single-entry system currently on the market is put out by Dome Publishing Company.

Pegboard Record-keeping System

The pegboard record-keeping system is actually a single-entry system because it requires only one entry per business transaction, but its unique design puts it in a category by itself. For one thing, it is an all-in-one system that not only keeps track of your records, but provides the materials for writing checks and issuing receipts. The system derives its name from its format. Checks and receipts are overlaid, one after another, on top of your permanent record sheets and held in place by pegs. Whenever you write a check or receipt, the information is automatically transferred, via carbon paper, to the record sheet below. This is the system's most distinguishing feature because it eliminates the cause of most accounting errors: forgetting to enter a transaction in the books. For more information on pegboard systems, check the yellow pages under "Business Forms and Systems" to locate the pegboard system specialists near you. Two of the leaders in this field are McBee and Safeguard.

Accountants and Bookkeepers

To determine which kind of record-keeping system is the most suitable for your consulting practice, we strongly recommend that you talk to an accountant. An accountant can help you choose the right system and set it up properly. Once the system is in place, you and the accountant should plan to meet at periodic intervals throughout the year to make sure that your records are in order and to evaluate your current financial position. To handle the day-to-day aspects of recordkeeping, you may also wish to use the services of a part-time bookkeeper, or you may prefer to do it yourself using one of the many accounting software packages that are available.

RECORDING YOUR INCOME

One of the most important functions of your record-keeping system is to provide an accurate record of the sources and amounts of income generated by your consulting practice. This is essential not only for tax-reporting purposes, but also for decision making. At the bare minimum, income records for your consulting practice must include a cash receipts journal and an accounts receivable journal.

Cash Receipts Journal

The sample cash receipts journal in Figure 14-1 illustrates how a consulting firm (in this case, a marketing research firm) can simply and easily keep track of its income flow. Recording the date, source, and amount of income earned, the cash receipts journal also indicates which services are most in demand. Thus, in addition to providing you with the income figures required by the IRS, it provides valuable information about your target market: the types of clients who are your best prospects. After a few months of recording your cash receipts in this way, you should know who your best clients are and which of your services are generating the most income.

The marketing research consulting firm in Figure 14-1 offers a variety of services: advertising effectiveness evaluation, consumer behavior studies, market share analysis, and product research. The cash receipts journal shows that the income from market share analysis far exceeds the income from any of the other consulting services. This is a good example of what marketing experts call the *80/20 rule*. According to the rule, 80 percent of a business's sales are likely to come from 20 percent of its customers (in this example, clients in the packaged-food industry). These are your best prospects, the clients who can most benefit from your services. Once you've identified them, you should direct your promotional, selling, and client-relations efforts toward filling their needs.

Figure 14-1 Cash Receipts Journal

	FERRIS AND ASSOCIATES APRIL 19XX CASH RECEIPTS JOURNAL				
Date	Description/Name	Advertising Evaluation	Consumer Behavior	Market Share Analysis	Product Research
4/1	Amalgamated Bakers			9 000–	
4/15	RPM Industries		3 000–		
4/20	Foremost Foods			7 500–	
4/30	Sierra Construction				6 000–

Accounts Receivable Journal

An accounts receivable journal, such as the one in Figure 14-2, serves much the same purpose as a cash receipts journal. Instead of showing the income you have already collected, though, it shows the money that is owed to you by clients, enabling you to keep track of outstanding accounts and to determine which clients are behind in their bills. When you receive payment, you can enter the income in your cash receipts journal.

BUSINESS EXPENSES

The record-keeping system you choose for your consulting practice must provide you with a record of tax-deductible business expenses. You will have to determine in advance precisely what expenses legitimately can be termed *business expenses*. The Internal Revenue Service regards as deductible only the expenses that are "ordinary

Figure 14-2 Accounts Receivable Journal

FERRIS AND ASSOCIATES **APRIL 19XX** **ACCOUNTS RECEIVABLE JOURNAL**					
Date Due	Description/ Name Date Rec'd	Amount Due	30 Days Past Due	60 Days Past Due	90 Days Past Due
3/15	Stevens Corporation	3 000–			
4/21	Foremost Foods 4/20	7 500–			
4/30	Sierra 4/30 Construction	6 000–			
5/17	Tanney Industries	4 000–			

in your business and necessary for its operation." Here are just a few of the expenses that meet these criteria:

Accounting services	Maintenance
Advertising	Materials
Attorney's fees	Membership fees
Automobile expenses	Messenger service
Business publications	Postage
Charitable contributions	Publicity
Consultants' fees	Rent
Credit reports	Safe-deposit box
Depreciation	Seminars
Entertainment	Stationery
Freight charges	Supplies
Insurance	Taxes
Interest	Travel
Licenses	Utilities

In calculating your business expenses, it's important to separate them from your personal expenses. For example, if you go on a trip for both business and pleasure, you can deduct only the business portion of the trip. If you decide to extend your stay for a vacation or make a nonbusiness side trip, you may not deduct the additional expenses. Along this same vein, if your spouse accompanies you on a business trip, you are normally not permitted to deduct his or her expenses for travel, meals, and lodging. (The exception to this is if you can prove that your spouse's presence serves a real business purpose as defined by the IRS.)

Cash Disbursements Journal

The best way to keep track of your expenses is to enter them in a cash disbursements journal like the one shown in Figure 14-3. Make sure to record the following information:

- Date expense was made
- Name of person or business receiving payment
- Check number
- Amount of check
- Category of business expense

When you set up your expense categories, arrange them in either alphabetical order or the order in which they will appear on your tax forms. This will make it easier for you to locate the information later and transfer it to your tax forms when preparing your income tax return. At the end of each month, it's also a good idea to add up the expenses in each category to determine exactly where your money is going. This should help you stay within your budget and keep unnecessary expenses to a minimum.

Automobile Expenses

If you use any automobiles or trucks in your consulting practice, expenses resulting from the business use of the vehicles are deduct-

Figure 14-3 Cash Disbursements Journal

FERRIS AND ASSOCIATES						
APRIL 19XX						
CASH DISBURSEMENTS JOURNAL						
Date	Description/ Name CK#		Accounting	Advertising	Automobile	Utilities
4/3	Mel Louis, C.P.A. 645		650–			
4/7	Daily Times 646			1 200–		
4/9	AutoDealer 647				350–	
4/13	Electric Company 648					110–

ible, including gasoline, oil, maintenance and repairs, insurance, depreciation, interest on car payments, parking fees, taxes, license fees, and tolls. When a motor vehicle is used for both business and personal purposes, you must divide your expenses between business and personal use.

There are two ways to calculate your deductible automobile expenses: (1) using a standard mileage rate and (2) deducting a percentage of the total operating costs.

Standard Mile Rate

To calculate your deductible expenses using this method, keep a record of all the miles your drive for business reasons during the year. Then multiply your total business mileage times the current rate allowed by the IRS. This will give you the dollar amount of your automobile expense:

Business miles
× Standard mileage rate
_____
Automobile expense (parking fees and
tolls may be added to this)

If you drive more than 15,000 business miles in any year, the standard mileage rate for each additional mile is reduced. Once you drive a vehicle 60,000 business miles, the standard mileage rate for all mileage for that vehicle drops again. The applicable rates are subject to change by the IRS.

Percentage of Total Operating Costs

To calculate your deductible expenses this way, keep a record of the number of miles you drive for business reasons during the year, and keep track of all of your automobile expenses. Then multiply the deductible percentage of automobile expenses times the total cost of operating your car:

$$\frac{12{,}000 \text{ business miles}}{20{,}000 \text{ total miles driven}} = 60\%$$

$5,000 (Total automobile operating costs)
× .60 (Deductible percentage)
_____
$3,000 (Automobile expense—parking fees
        and tolls may be added to this sum)

Because this method is based on your automobile operating costs rather than on a standard rate per mile, it's especially important to keep receipts documenting your automobile expenses.

To make sure that you are claiming the full automobile deduction the IRS allows, you should try both methods (at least in the beginning). Then, after comparing the totals, choose the method that gives you the higher deduction.

Entertainment Expenses

Business entertainment expenses are tax deductible subject to the limits and rules currently imposed by the IRS. To qualify as a deductible item, the entertainment expense must be ordinary and necessary in performing your consulting duties or operating your business. As with your automobile expenses, you must separate your business entertainment expenses from the nonbusiness ones.

To determine whether an entertainment expense is deductible, ask yourself if the entertainment had a clear business purpose. Was it to get new business or to encourage the continuation of an existing business relationship? If your answer is yes, you should be able to claim the expense as a business deduction. For example, taking a prospective client to lunch or dinner is a deductible expense if you discuss business at some time during the meal.

To comply with the IRS rules on entertainment, you should keep a record of all business entertainment expenses, along with the receipts or other supporting evidence to back them up. Entering a luncheon date on your desk calendar isn't enough. To be properly documented, the lunch must be backed up by the receipt for the meal.

When claiming an expense as a business entertainment deduction, you must be able to prove the following:

- Amount of expense
- Date entertainment took place
- Location of the entertainment, such as a restaurant or theater
- Reason for the entertainment (to promote your consulting services, to discuss a consulting project)
- Name and title (or occupation) of each person you entertained

The more specific you can be, the better because this will add to the validity of your deductions.

Reimbursable Client Expenses

You should keep separate records of the client-related expenses for which you will be reimbursed by the client. For example, a travel expense reimbursement form (Figure 14-4) provides a record of travel expenses incurred on the client's behalf. These expenses should be billed directly to the client's account in addition to your consulting fees. Because the client is reimbursing you for the expenses, you may not deduct them from your taxes. However, the client may be entitled to do so.

YOUR TAXES

Much as you might like to ignore them, taxes are an inevitable part of doing business. If you keep good records, taxes shouldn't pose a problem for you. The nature of your consulting practice, its legal form, and its location will determine the taxes you must pay.

Federal Taxes

The two best-known federal taxes that entrepreneurs are required to pay are income tax and self-employment tax. If you employ other people in your consulting practice, you may also be subject to employment taxes.

Income Tax

Every business is required by law to file an annual income tax return. The form you use depends on whether your consulting firm is a sole proprietorship, a partnership, or a corporation.

If you are a sole proprietorship, you should report your business income and deductions on Schedule C (Form 1040). Attach this schedule to your individual tax return (Form 1040) and submit them together. If you own more than one business, you must file a separate Schedule C for each one.

Figure 14-4 Travel Expense Reimbursement Form

Ferris and Associates
Marketing Research

TRAVEL EXPENSE REIMBURSEMENT FORM

Client's Name _____ Consulting Project _____

Address _____

	Date	
EXPENSE	Place	
Airfare		
Car Rental		
Tolls		
Gasoline		
Taxi		
Breakfast		
Lunch		
Dinner		
Hotel		
Telephone		
Tips		
Misc.		

Submitted by _____ Approved by _____

Date _____ Date _____

If you are a partner in a consulting firm, your income and deductions from the partnership should be reported on Schedule K-1 (Form 1065) and filed along with your individual tax return. Each of your partners should do the same, accounting for his or her income and deductions in this way. In addition, the total income and deductions for the partnership itself must be reported on Form 1065.

A corporation reports its taxable income on Form 1120. S corporations use Form 1120S. Any income or dividends that you receive from the corporation should be entered on your individual tax return. However, if you are a shareholder in an S corporation, your income and deductions should be reported in the same way that they would be in a partnership. In this instance, you use Schedule K-1 (Form 1120S).

Self-employment Tax

Self-employment tax is a Social Security tax for people who are self-employed. It's similar to the Social Security tax paid by wage earners, but you pay it yourself instead of having it withheld from your paycheck. To find out more about this tax, check IRS publication 533, "Self-Employment Tax."

Estimated Tax

The IRS requires that you pay your income and self-employment taxes each year on a pay-as-you-go basis. Rather than paying them in one lump sum at the end of the tax period, you must pay them in installments by these dates:

- April 15
- June 15
- September 15
- January 15 (of the following year)

You pay one-quarter of your total tax liability on each date until the liability is paid in full. If you discover in, say, August that you are paying too much or too little tax, you can decrease or increase the size of the remaining payment accordingly. You are required to prepay at least 90 percent of your tax liability each year. If you prepay less, you may be subject to a penalty.

Try to make your estimates as accurate as possible to spare yourself that expense. When in doubt, you will do better to pay more than the amount you've estimated so as to ensure meeting the 90 percent prepayment minimum. The form you use to estimate your tax is Form 1040-ES, which can be obtained from the IRS.

Employment Taxes

If you have employees in your consulting practice, you will probably need to pay employment taxes. These taxes include the following:

- Federal income tax, which you withhold from your employees' wages
- Social Security tax, part of which you withhold from your employees' wages and the rest of which you contribute as an employer
- Federal unemployment tax, which you as an employer must pay

Report both the income tax and the Social Security tax on Form 941, and pay both taxes when you submit the forms. Report and pay the federal unemployment tax separately, using Form 940. For more information about employment tax and which ones, if any, you must pay, read IRS publication 15, "Circular E."

State and Local Taxes

The types and amounts of state and local taxes that you, as a business owner, must pay depend on where your consulting firm is located. For instance, businesses in New York and California are subject to higher rates of taxation than those in Pennsylvania and

Texas. Some states have income and sales taxes; others don't. All states have unemployment taxes.

Just as the states vary when it comes to taxation, so do counties, cities, and towns within the states. Some of the taxes imposed at this level include business taxes, licensing fees, and income taxes.

To make sure that your consulting firm is meeting its state and local tax obligations, contact the authorities for your locality to determine the taxes for which you are responsible.

For more information on business taxation, refer to the IRS publications described in Chapter 15.

15

Using Outside Support Services

Prospective consultants are often surprised to learn that more than 50 percent of all consulting firms are one-person operations. Even when others are employed in the business, consulting practices by their very nature tend to be small, with 25 percent of all firms ranging in size from 2 to 10 people. In most instances, owners are directly involved not only in carrying out consulting assignments, but also in conducting a major portion of the activities associated with running a business. How do they do everything? By using outside support services.

There are many outside services that are willing and eager to help your consulting firm succeed. Whether you need help in obtaining financing, keeping your books in order, or designing a brochure to promote your business, or you simply want someone to type your letters or answer your phone, help is available.

TYPES OF SUPPORT SERVICES

Here are some of the individuals and institutions that you can turn to for help when you need it:

Accountants	Government agencies
Answering services	Insurance agents
Attorneys	Libraries
Bankers	Temporary-help services
Brochure specialists	Trade and professional
Chambers of commerce	associations
Colleges and universities	Word-processing services
Consultants	

Each of these support services can provide you with information and assistance that otherwise might not be readily accessible to your consulting firm.

Accountants

An accountant can be instrumental in helping you keep your consulting firm operating on a sound financial basis. Even if you are already familiar with record-keeping procedures or employ a part-time bookkeeper to maintain your records, you may still be able to benefit from the services of an outside accountant. In addition to designing an accounting system that's suitable for your specific needs, an accountant can assist in the following tasks:

- Determining cash requirements
- Budgeting
- Forecasting
- Controlling costs
- Preparing financial statements
- Interpreting financial data
- Obtaining loans
- Preparing tax returns

You can find public accountants listed in the yellow pages of the telephone directory, but for the best results it's advisable to try to locate one through a personal recommendation. Another approach is to obtain the name of an accountant through one of the national or state accounting associations. The following are two of the larger associations:

American Institute of Certified Public Accountants
1211 Avenue of the Americas
New York, NY 10036

National Society of Public Accountants
1010 N. Fairfax St.
Alexandria, VA 22314

Answering Services

One of a consulting firm's strongest assets can be a good answering service. Aside from answering your phone and relaying messages, an answering service can help you work more efficiently by screening callers or paging you when you are out of the office. By answering your phone in a courteous and professional manner, an answering service enhances your credibility as a consultant. Unfortunately, though, not all answering services are created equal. If you decide to use an answering service, *listen* to the various services available and compare how they respond to callers. Then choose the service that is most in keeping with the type of image you want to project.

To keep your costs down while still creating a professional image, be sure to look into the answering services available through your telephone carrier. These often provide a nice compromise between using an answering machine and hiring an outside service to handle your calls.

Attorneys

An attorney can be useful in your consulting firm from the beginning, helping you determine which legal form is best for you, preparing and filing the necessary paperwork to get started, and so on. Once your business is under way, you may need an attorney from time to time to interpret legal documents, draw up contracts, or represent you in court. The best way to find an attorney is through business acquaintances, your accountant, or your banker. The state bar association also can provide you with the names of attorneys in your area.

Bankers

Your banker can be a valuable business ally, providing a variety of financial information, advice, and services. These include helping you prepare financial reports, obtain a line of credit, transfer funds, bill customers, and more. In addition, because bankers come into contact with many different segments of the community, your banker may be in a position to hear news that affects your consulting firm before you do.

The time to begin establishing a good working relationship with your banker is *before* you need a loan. Start by making an appointment to meet the manager of the branch where your banking transactions will take place. The purpose of this meeting is to open a channel of communication between the two of you. Rather than just being another number on a ledger, you want to differentiate your account from the others. Providing the banker with a brief summary of your background and business objectives can add another dimension to the facts already on paper. You might also offer to keep the banker posted on the progress of your consulting firm by sending your financial reports to the bank on a regular basis.

Brochure Specialists

A brochure specialist can help you design and produce the type of brochure that will effectively promote your consulting services. Brochure specialists know how to

- Write and edit copy
- Create graphics
- Arrange the layout of a brochure
- Deal with printers

If yours is one of the many consulting fields in which a well-designed brochure is practically a prerequisite for obtaining new clients, you should consider using this type of support service. You can find brochure specialists by looking in the yellow pages under "Advertising—Direct Mail" and "Graphic Designers" or by checking with the printers in your area.

Chambers of Commerce

As a consultant, it can be to your advantage to utilize the resources of your local chamber of commerce. The traditional role of each chamber is to represent the business interests of its community and to promote the area's economy. In addition to providing you with marketing information and other data, the chamber can be a means of making business contacts and obtaining client referrals. To find out more about the various services available to you through the chamber of commerce, contact the chapter in your community.

Colleges and Universities

Colleges and universities are another support service that shouldn't be overlooked. Educational institutions offer access to information, skills, and training through

- Libraries, containing books, periodicals, government reports, reference works, maps, charts, and audiovisual aids
- Professors who are knowledgeable in a variety of business-related areas
- Labor, in the form of students who are receiving training in your field

- Additional education, in the form of classes in management theory, business operations, advertising methods, and other related areas
- Seminars designed especially for small business owners (often sponsored by the Small Business Administration)

Consultants

Sometimes what a consultant needs is the services of another consultant. For example, a marketing consultant can help you research potential markets and develop a promotional strategy for selling your services. A government procurement consultant can assist you in obtaining government contracts. A data-processing consultant can improve your ability to store and retrieve information. Whatever your needs, there is likely to be a consultant who can fulfill them.

Government Agencies

Agencies of the government at the local, state, and federal levels can provide you with an abundance of useful information at little or no cost. The following are among the agencies whose services you might want to use.

Department of Commerce.   This department oversees the research and distribution of economic information, which is available to the public in the form of publications and reports. These include

- *Survey of Current Business*, a monthly periodical that provides updates on changes in the nation's economy and the levels of business production and distribution
- *Census Bureau Reports*, covering such topics as population statistics (age, income, level of education, family status, and other demographic data) and manufacturing, business, and agricultural trends

In addition to these reports, Commerce Department specialists can advise you in such specific areas as domestic and foreign marketing opportunities, contacting foreign representatives, and deciphering tariff and trade regulations. To find the DOC office closest to you, check the phone directory white pages under "United States Government" or write to the Department of Commerce in Washington, D.C.

Economic Development Offices.   Many communities maintain their own economic development offices, which consultants can utilize. They differ from chambers of commerce in that they are maintained by local governments rather than local businesses. They can provide you with current statistical data regarding the economy, building activity, sales trends, labor force, wages and salaries, banking, community services, and so on.

Government Printing Office.   This organization oversees the publication and distribution of government documents, pamphlets, reports, and books on a variety of subjects, many of which are directly related to business. Depending on the type of consulting work you do, some of these publications may be of interest to you. To receive a catalog of the publications available, write to the U.S. Government Printing Office, Superintendent of Documents, Washington, DC 20402.

Internal Revenue Service.   The IRS can answer any questions you have concerning your federal income taxes. Tax specialists in local IRS offices can handle specific questions, or you can refer to any of their numerous guides and publications. One particularly valuable guide is the *Tax Guide for Small Businesses,* which is updated annually. It contains approximately 200 pages of information covering books and records, accounting periods, determining gross profit, deductible expenses, depreciation, and other topics. This publication is available free of charge at your local IRS office. Some of the other IRS publications you can obtain are listed later in this chapter.

Small Business Administration.   The SBA is designed to aid small businesses by helping them obtain financing, providing them with management and technical assistance, conducting business seminars and workshops, and assisting in procuring government contracts (see Chapter 11).

This assistance is achieved through the operation of field offices, the distribution of publications, and the activities of the Service Corps of Retired Executives (SCORE) and the Active Corps of Executives (ACE), volunteer groups of professionals who assist the SBA in advising small businesses. A sampling of the publications produced by the SBA appears later in this chapter, along with the addresses of the SBA field offices.

Small Business Development Centers.   For advice on how to run your consulting business better, develop a business plan, generate leads and referrals, obtain information about government programs, and more, check to see if there is a small business development center (SBDC) near you. Located throughout the United States, SBDCs, which are usually affiliated with a college or university, offer one-on-one counseling to entrepreneurs in such areas as management, marketing, accounting, finance, and computers. Serving the needs of both prospective and current entrepreneurs, SBDCs can assist consultants through each stage of starting and running their businesses.

Insurance Agents

The importance of insurance and the different types of coverage available were discussed in Chapter 3. An insurance agent can analyze your consulting firm's specific needs and help you obtain adequate coverage. Aspects of risk management that you should discuss with your agent include how to protect your assets, workers, and earnings. The best ways to find an insurance agent are through recommendations and comparison shopping. Talking to more than one agent not only lets you evaluate the levels of coverage and costs of different plans, but also gives you an idea of which agent is the most knowledgeable about your type of business.

Libraries

Much of the information that consultants need to operate their businesses can be obtained free of charge from libraries. It can be found not only in books, but also in the assortment of magazines, newspapers, reference works, government publications, maps, charts, and audiovisual aids that are available. Technical explanations, statistical data, industry updates, trends, and economic forecasts are just some of the subject areas in which you can find information. In addition to the public libraries, there are specialized libraries sponsored by colleges and universities; private industry, trade, and professional associations; labor unions; and research centers.

Temporary-Help Services

On occasions when you need outside help to stay on top of the work load or complete a project, a temporary-help service is the answer. It can provide well-qualified, temporary help on a moment's notice. Whether you need a typist, bookkeeper, editor, researcher, or other clerical or professional help, a temporary-help service should be able to meet your personnel requirements. As an added bonus, temporary-help services take care of screening, interviewing, and testing applicants and checking their references.

Trade and Professional Associations

Trade and professional associations—organizations whose members are in the same industry or perform the same services—can be particularly helpful to consultants. Both types of associations are concerned with helping their members become more productive and cope with business problems. In many instances, professional associations set the standards for their fields, formulating codes of ethics and advocating certain policies and procedures. It's not uncommon for trade and professional associations to offer assistance in such areas as accounting, promotion, public relations, and research. The majority of associations also have ongoing government relations programs, thus enabling members to have a collective voice in communicating with the government. Through their meetings and seminars, associations make it possible for individuals to come into contact with others in the field.

To obtain information on trade and professional associations or to find out which ones represent consultants in your particular field, write to

American Society of Association Executives
1575 Eye St. N.W.
Washington, DC 20005

Two other sources of information, which are available at most public libraries, are these directories: *National Trade and Professional Associations of the United States* (Washington, DC: Columbia Books) and the *Encyclopedia of Associations*, Vol. 1: *National Organizations of the U.S.* (Detroit: Gale Research Co.). Both are updated periodically.

Word-Processing Services

The widespread availability of personal computers has resulted in a growing number of word-processing services. They can be invaluable to you as a consultant, helping you produce professional-looking proposals and reports, handle correspondence, and create direct-mail materials to promote your business. In addition to general word processing, many services specialize in meeting the needs of those in the legal, medical, financial, engineering, and academic fields. To locate word-processing services in your vicinity, check the yellow pages under "Word Processing."

GOVERNMENT PUBLICATIONS

The following is a sampling of the publications that have been prepared by the Internal Revenue Service and the Small Business Administration.

Internal Revenue Service Publications

Title	No.
Your Rights as a Taxpayer	1
Employer's Tax Guide (Circular E)	15
Your Federal Income Tax	17
Tax Guide for Small Business	334
Fuel Tax Credits and Refunds	378
Travel, Entertainment, and Gift Expenses	463
Tax Withholding and Estimated Tax	505
Excise Taxes	510
Taxable and Nontaxable Income	525
Charitable Contributions	526
Miscellaneous Deductions	529
Self-employment Tax	533
Depreciation	534
Business Expenses	535
Net Operating Losses	536
Accounting Periods and Methods	538
Tax Information on Partnerships	541
Tax Information on Corporations	542
Sales and Other Dispositions of Assets	544
Investment Income and Expenses	550
Basis of Assets	551
Recordkeeping for Individuals	552
Retirement Plans for the Self-employed	560
Taxpayers Starting a Business	583
Business Use of Your Home	587
Tax Information on S Corporations	589
Individual Retirement Arrangements (IRAs)	590
Understanding the Collection Process	594
Guide to Free Tax Services	910
Tax Information for Direct Sellers	911
Business Use of a Car	917
Employment Taxes and Information Returns	937
How to Begin Depreciating Your Property	946
Per Diem Rates	1542

Small Business Administration Publications

SMALL BUSINESS ADMINISTRATION OFFICES

Central Office
U.S. Small Business Administration
409 Third St., S.W.
Washington, DC 20416
800-827-5722

Regional Offices

Region I
155 Federal St.
9th Floor
Boston, MA 02110
617-451-2023

Region II
26 Federal Plaza
Room 31-08
New York, NY 10278
212-264-1450

Region III
Allendale Square
475 Allendale Rd.
Suite 201
King of Prussia, PA 19406
215-962-3700

Region IV
1375 Peachtree St., N.E.
Atlanta, GA 30367-8102
404-347-2797

Region V
300 S. Riverside Plaza
Suite 1975
Chicago, IL 60606-6617
312-353-5000

Region VI
8625 King George Dr.
Building C
Dallas, TX 75235-3391
214-767-7633

Region VII
911 Walnut St.
Kansas City, MO 64106
816-426-3608

Region VIII
633 17th St.
Denver, CO 80202
303-294-7186

Region IX
71 Stevenson St.
San Francisco, CA 94105-2939
415-744-6402

Region X
2601 Fourth Ave.
Suite 440
Seattle, WA 98121-1273
206-553-5676

Index